AN

ELEMENTARY COPTIC GRAMMAR

OF THE

SAHIDIC DIALECT

BY

C. C. WALTERS

B.A., Ph.D.

Lady Wallis Budge
Research Fellow in Egyptology
University College, Oxford

OXFORD
B. H. BLACKWELL
M·CM·LXXII

Printed by Blackwell's in the City of Oxford.

Corrigenda

p.15, § 32 e) i); for ϣⲙⲛ̄ⲧ ⲛ̄ϣⲉ read ϣⲙⲛ̄ⲧ ϣⲉ

p.15, § 32 e) ii); for ⲥⲁϣϥ̄ ⲛ̄ⳍⲉ read ⲥⲁϣϥ̄ ⲛ̄ϣⲉ

p.38, § 69; for ϣⲁⲛⲧⲟⲩⲧⲙ̄ ⲗⲁⲁⲩ read ϣⲁⲛⲧⲟⲩⲧⲙ̄ⲕⲁ ⲗⲁⲁⲩ

p.45, Vocabulary; for 'repentence' read 'repentance'

p. 72, § 121 i), 1.4: for ⲁⳅⲉⲛⲧⲟⲡⲟⲥ ⲭⲓⲣⲱⲙⲉ ⲛ̄ⳝ read

ⲁⳅⲉⲛⲧⲟⲡⲟⲥ ⲭⲓⲣⲱⲙⲉ ⲛ̄ⲥⲟⲛ̄

CONTENTS

§§ 1- 4	The Alphabet	1- 3
§§ 5-14	**Pronouns and Possessives**	3
§§ 5- 6	Suffix Pronouns	3- 4
§§ 7- 8	Independent Pronouns	4- 5
§ 9	Pronouns of Emphasis or Contrast	5
§ 10	The Possessive Article	5
§ 11	The Possessive Pronoun	6
§ 12	The Possessive Adjective	6- 7
§ 13	The Demonstrative Pronoun	7- 8
§ 14	Interrogative Pronouns (cross-ref.)	8
§§ 15-17	**Nouns**	8
§ 15	Gender	8
§ 16	Plural Forms	9
§ 17	Compound Nouns	9-10
§§ 18-24	**The Article**	10
§§ 18-22	The Definite Article	10-12
§§ 23-24	The Indefinite Article	12
§§ 25-26	**The Genitive**	12-13
§§ 27-31	**The Adjective**	13-14
§§ 32-40	**Numerals**	14
§§ 32-35	Cardinals	14-16
§§ 36-38	Ordinals	16-17
§ 39	Dating (note)	17
§ 40	Numerical value of alphabet (note)	17
§§ 41-48	**Non-Verbal Sentences**	17
§§ 42-44	With nominal predicate	17-19
§ 45	With adverbial predicate	20
§ 46	No non-verbal future	20
§ 47	Negation	21
§ 48	Conclusion	21
	Exercise 1	21-23

§§	49–79	<u>The Verb</u>	23
§	50	The Infinitive	23–24
§	51	The Qualitative	24
§	52	Verbal classes (note)	24
§§	53–56	The Suffix Conjugation	24–26
		Exercise II	27–28
§	57	The Prefix Conjugation (introduction)	28
§	58	1st Present	29
§	59	1st Perfect	29–30
§	60	Imperfect	30
§	61	1st Habitude	30–31
§	62	1st Future	31
§	63	3rd Future	32
§§	64–65	Potential Future	32–33
§	66	The Optative	34
§	67	Future Imperfect	34–35
		Exercise III	35–37
§§	68–69	ⲩⲁⲛⲧⲉ-	38
§	70	ⲙ̄ⲡⲁⲧⲉ-	38
§§	71–73	The Conjunctive	39–40
§	74	The Second Tenses	41–42
§	75	Circumstantial Tenses	42
§	76	The Circumstantial Present	42–43
§	77	The Future Circumstantial	43–44
§	78	Tenses with ⲛⲉ-	44
§	79	The Imperative	44–45
		Exercise IV	45–47
§§	80–85	<u>The Infinitives</u>	48
§	81	The Simple Infinitive	48–49
§§	82–83	The Causative Infinitive	49–50
§	84	Negation	50
§	85	The Potential Infinitive	50
§	86	<u>The Passive</u>	51
§	87	<u>Prepositions</u>	51–52

	Exercise V	52–54
§§ 88–97	The Verbal Sentence	55
§§ 88–92	Word order, variations and emphasis	55–56
§§ 93–95	Direct and indirect object	56–57
§ 96	The Adverb	57
§ 97	Speech	57
	Exercise VI	58–59
§§ 98–109	Questions	59
§§ 98–105	Interrogative adverbs and pronouns	59–61
§§ 107–108	Interrogative particles	62–63
§ 109	Double questions	63
	Exercise VII	63–64
§§ 110–116	Conditional Sentences	64
§ 111	Real Conditional Sentences	65–67
§ 112	Artificial Conditional Sentences	67–68
§§ 113–116	Notes on conditional sentences	68
	Exercise VIII	69–70
§§ 117–119	Temporal Clauses	70
§ 117	Contemporaneous temporal clauses	70
§ 118	Past temporal clauses	71
§ 119	Future temporal clauses	71
§ 120	Causal Clauses	72
§ 121	Final Clauses	72
§§ 122–128	Relative Clauses	73
§§ 123–126	Antecedent and subject of relative clause similar	73–75
§ 127	Antecedent and subject of relative clause different	75–77
§ 128	The Relative Substantive	77
	Summary table of relative constructions	78
	Exercise IX	79–80
§ 129	Negation – summary	81

PREFACE

The aims of this work are limited. As its title suggests, it does not pretend to be an exhaustive study of the Coptic language, although a fundamental reappraisal of the subject is becoming an urgent necessity. Rather is it an attempt to present the basic structure of Coptic grammar in as succinct a manner as possible, the dialect chosen for this task being Sahidic, the principal literary tongue. It is intended primarily for those coming fresh to the language and wishing to obtain a painless introduction to its fundamentals. For more advanced and detailed guidance the student should then refer to W. Till's Koptische Grammatik, and with this in mind I have, throughout the grammar, given the relevant paragraph references to Till in brackets at the head of each section.

Within the limited compass of this grammar I have tried to incorporate the principal advances in our knowledge of Coptic that have occurred since the publication in 1948 of J.M. Plumley's invaluable Introductory Coptic Grammar. However, the student is strongly urged to follow up the references to articles and books in order to understand the new ideas more fully.

In the preparation of this work I have received the encouragement and assistance of many, and to them all I now publicly express my sincere thanks. I hope very much that co-operation will not cease here, and that others will make their suggestions and criticisms known.

In the exercises I have occasionally inserted a comma where the original text would have had no punctuation. Finally, an impassioned plea to the student that he should learn how to use Crum's Dictionary as soon as possible; there is no substitute.

C. Walters
Oxford 1972

Biblical references are by chapter and verse, others by page and line.

Besa: K.H. Kuhn, Letters and Sermons of Besa; Corpus Scriptorum
Christianorum Orientalium (C.S.C.O.) Vols. 157 & 158

Budge M.T.: W. Budge, Miscellaneous Coptic Texts in the Dialect of
Upper Egypt (1915)

Budge Martyrdoms: W. Budge, Coptic Martyrdoms in the Dialect of Upper
Egypt (1915)

Cha: M. Chaine, Le manuscrit de la version copte en dialecte
sahidique des 'Apophthegmata Patrum' (1960)

C.L.: J. Drescher, Three Coptic Legends (Supplement aux Annales
du Service, Cahier 4, 1947)

Gen.: Genesis

H.M.: W. Till, Koptische Heiligen- und Martyrerlegenden (Orientalia
christiana analecta 102 and 108, 1935 & 1936)

Josh.: Joshua, in H. Thompson, A Coptic Palimpsest (1911)

P. Cod.: W. Crum, Der Papyruscodex saec. VI – VII (1915)

Pro.: W. Worrell, The Proverbs of Solomon (1931)

Ps.: Psalms; W. Budge, The Earliest Known Coptic Psalter (1898)

Ru.: Ruth, in H. Thompson, op. cit.

Sh.: J. Leipoldt, Sinuthii Archimandritae: Vita et Opera Omnia
(C.S.C.O., Vols. 42 and 73)

St. A.: G. Garitte, S. Antonii Vitae (C.S.C.O., Vol. 117)

Ste.: G. Steindorff, Koptische Grammatik (Lesestücke) (1894)

Till: W. Till, Koptische Grammatik (Lesestücke) (1960)

Several volumes of the Coptic Version of the New Testament are also quoted:
Acts (Vol. VI); Jo: John (Vol. III); Lk: Luke (Vol. II); Mk: Mark (Vol. 1);
Mt: Matthew (Vol. 1)

Journals: J.N.E.S. Journal of Near Eastern Studies

INTRODUCTION

A Origins

The word 'Copt' is derived from the Arabic <u>qibt</u>, which in turn is a corruption of the Greek word for 'Egyptian – αἰγύπτιος. Thus, although the Arabic word was applied to a people who by that time were predominantly Christian (the Arab conquest of Egypt occurred in 641 A.D.), it must be realised that in origin the word had no connection with Christianity, but was used to designate the descendants of the Ancient Egyptian race as opposed to the foreign elements living in the country. That 'Copt' and 'Christian' later became virtually synonymous must not obscure this fact.

Similarly, it must not be thought that the Coptic language was a preserve of the Christian communities of Egypt, a language that manifested itself with the conversion of the country to the new faith.[1] Chronologically, the emergence of Coptic and the coming of Christianity are closely linked, but the earliest texts we possess employing the new script make it clear that it originated among non-Christians.[2] These texts, dating to the latter part of the 1st or the first half of the 2nd centuries A.D., are written in what is known as 'Old Coptic'. This script seems to have been the child of necessity. The hieroglyphic and demotic systems were becoming increasingly unsatisfactory vehicles of expression. This was especially true where the exact pronunciation of words was all-important – with magical texts, for example, which form the bulk of our Old Coptic library. Old Coptic was thus developed, using the Greek alphabet and incorporating certain letters borrowed from Demotic to represent sounds not catered for by the Greek. It should be noted that the Old Coptic texts employed more Demotic letters than the language in its later form, where the number was seven.[3]

---

1 See P.E. Kahle: <u>Bala'izah</u>, Vol. 1, (Oxford 1954), p.252ff.; W. Till: 'Coptic and Its Value', in <u>Bulletin of the John Rylands Library</u>, Vol.40, p.229ff. 2 Kahle, <u>op. cit.</u> p.252 for refs. 3 Kahle, <u>op. cit.</u> p.244, note 1.

Christianity penetrated Egypt at first through the Greek-dominated cities and towns such as Alexandria. At the beginning, therefore, Greek would have been a satisfactory medium for the transmission of the new religion. But with the passage of time the need to facilitate missionary work among the native Egyptians, and to provide a version of the Scriptures intelligible to these people, led to the adoption and development of the Coptic language. This process must have been under way by the end of the 3rd century, although fully standardised Coptic texts do not appear before the 4th century.[4] After 641 A.D. Arabic gradually replaced Coptic, and by the 16th century it had died out as a spoken language. It is still used today in church services, but in association with Arabic, and it seems only a matter of time before it disappears altogether, thus severing our last link, however tenuous, with Ancient Egypt.

B **Dialects**[5]

The Coptic language was not homogeneous. The sources, spread and interrelationships of the various dialects are still a matter of some dispute. At present, five principal dialects are recognised, each deriving from the speech of a particular locality.

a) <u>Sahidic</u> Signified by the letter S in dictionaries etc; earlier known as Theban. The classical form of the language, eventually used throughout Egypt, though probably Upper Egyptian in origin.[6]

b) <u>Bohairic</u> (B) Earlier known as Memphite. The dialect used in Coptic churches today. It is generally considered to have been centred in the Delta, though this has been disputed.[7]

c) <u>Akhmimic</u> (A) From the region of Akhmim.

d) <u>Sub-Akhmimim</u> (A^2) Exact locality uncertain, possibly around Assiut.

e) <u>Fayumic</u> (F) From the Fayum.

4 Kahle, <u>op. cit.</u>, pp.260-263. 5 Kahle, <u>op. cit.</u>, p.193ff. 6 Kahle, <u>op. cit.</u>, p.233ff. 7 Kahle, <u>op. cit.</u> pp.251-252.

I THE ALPHABET

1 The letters in brackets indicate the approximate phonetic values.

  a) 24 Greek letters: Ⲁ (a): Ⲃ (b): Ⲅ (g): Ⲇ (d): Ⲉ (ē):
     Ⲍ (z): Ⲏ (ē): Ⲑ (th): Ⲓ (i,j): Ⲕ (k): Ⲗ (l):
     Ⲙ (m): Ⲛ (n): Ⲝ (ks): Ⲟ (ŏ): Ⲡ (p): Ⲣ (r): Ⲥ (s):
     Ⲧ (t): Ⲩ (w,u,y): Ⲫ (ph): Ⲭ (kh): Ⲯ (ps): Ⲱ (ō)

  b) 6 letters from Demotic: ϣ (sh): ϥ (f): ϩ (h): ϫ (j):
     ϭ (ğ): ϯ (ti)

2 <u>Notes on the alphabet</u>

  a) The letters Ⲅ , Ⲇ , and Ⲍ normally appear only in Greek words
     employed in the Coptic vocabulary, though Ⲅ can appear for Ⲕ after
     Ⲛ , e.g. ⲚⲄ- for ⲚⲔ̄- (2nd person singular, Conjunctive tense,
     p.39).

  b) The letters Ⲑ , Ⲝ , Ⲫ , Ⲯ and Ⲭ can appear as abbreviations
     for ⲦϨ , ⲔⲤ , ⲠϨ , ⲠⲤ and ⲔϨ , exx. ⲐⲈⲚⲈⲈⲦⲈ for ⲦϨⲈⲚⲈⲈⲦⲈ 'the
     monastery'; ⲐⲈ for ⲦϨⲈ 'the way'; ⲜⲞⲨⲣ for ⲔⲤⲞⲨⲣ 'finger-ring';
     ⲪⲀⲠ for ⲠϨⲀⲠ 'the judgement'.

  c) Words beginning with the letter ϯ appear in dictionaries under Ⲧ .

  d) All the letters, with the exception of ϣ , ϫ , ϩ , ϭ and ϯ ,
     could have numerical value (see <u>Plumley</u>, § 116).

3 <u>The Consonants</u> (T. § 30ff)

  a) In the following instances <u>only</u> the letter Ⲛ changes to Ⲙ before
     Ⲙ , Ⲡ , Ⲯ and Ⲫ :

    i) as the genitive (p.12), exx. ⲠⲤⲀϨ Ⲙ̄ⲠⲒⲎⲖ 'the teacher of Israel'
      (Jo. 3.10) ⲦⲈϨⲒⲎ Ⲙ̄ⲠⲬⲞⲈⲒⲤ 'the way of the Lord' (Jo. 1.23)
      ⲠⲤⲰⲦⲎⲣ Ⲙ̄ⲠⲔⲟⲤⲘⲟⲤ 'the saviour of the world' (Jo. 4.42)

    ii) as the negative (p.28ff.), exx Ⲙ̄ⲠϨⲘ̄ϨⲀⲖ ⲤⲞⲞⲨⲚ ⲀⲚ 'the servant
      does not know' (Jo. 15.15) ⲘⲎ Ⲙ̄ⲠⲀⲒ ⲀⲚ ⲠⲈ Ⲓ̄Ⲥ̄ 'is this not Jesus?'
      (Jo. 6.42)

    iii) as the plural <u>definite</u> article (p.10ff), exx. Ⲙ̄ⲘⲀⲐⲎⲦⲎⲤ
      Ⲙ̄ⲘⲰⲨⲤⲎⲤ 'the disciples of Moses' (Jo. 9.28) Ⲙ̄ⲘⲈⲈⲨⲈ
      Ⲙ̄ⲠⲈϤϨⲎⲦ 'the thoughts of his heart' (Ps. 32.11)

iv)   as the dative (p.51), exx. ⲡⲉϫⲁⲩ ⲙ̄ⲫⲓⲗⲓⲡⲡⲟⲥ 'he said to Philip'
(Jo. 6.5) ⲁϥⲧⲁⲁⲥ ⲙ̄ⲡϣⲏⲣⲉ 'he gave it to the Son' (Jo. 5.22)

v)   as the adjectival ⲛ̄ (p.13), exx. ⲍⲁⲍ ⲙ̄ⲙⲁⲑⲏⲧⲏⲥ 'many disciples'
(Jo. 3.26) ⲟⲩⲛⲟϭ ⲙ̄ⲙⲏⲛϣⲉ 'a great multitude' (Jo. 6.5) ⲡⲟⲉⲓⲕ ⲙ̄ⲙⲉ
'the true bread' (Jo. 6.32)

vi)   the preposition ⲛ̄ and all other prepositions ending with the
letter ⲛ̄ , except ⲙⲛ̄ (p.51), exx. ⲍⲓⲧⲙ̄ ⲡⲛⲟⲩⲧⲉ 'from God'
(Jo. 3.2) ⲍⲓϫⲙ̄ ⲡⲉⲓⲧⲟⲟⲩ 'upon this mountain' (Jo. 4.20) <u>But</u>
ⲙⲛ̄ ⲙⲁⲣⲑⲁ 'and Martha' (Jo. 11.1)

vii)   when introducing the indirect object (p.56ff), exx. ⲡⲉⲓⲱⲧ ⲙⲉ
ⲙ̄ⲡϣⲏⲣⲉ 'the Father loveth the Son' (Jo. 5.20) ⲃⲱⲗ ⲉⲃⲟⲗ ⲙ̄ⲡⲉⲓⲣ̄ⲡⲉ
'overthrow this temple' (Jo. 2.19)

There are two occasions on which the above rules do not apply.

i)   ⲛ does <u>not</u> change before an ⲙ when the latter is functioning
as a sonant consonant, i.e. where pronunciation inserts a vowel
sound between the two letters, though this is not written, e.g.
ⲛⲙ̄ⲥⲁⲍ not ⲙ̄ⲙ̄ⲥⲁⲍ 'the crocodiles'. Experience will indicate
when this applies. In this grammar and elsewhere it is usual
for the sonant properties of a consonant to be indicated by a
superlinear stroke, though some publications, including Crum's
Dictionary, omit this feature. The five principal sonant consonants are ⲃ , ⲗ , ⲙ , ⲛ and ⲣ .

ii)   Similarly, an ⲛ will not change before an ⲙ if this ⲙ is itself
an ⲛ that has been altered. Thus, in the expression ⲛ̄ⲙ̄ⲙⲁⲁϫⲉ
the initial ⲛ̄ is introducing an indirect object, and since it
stands before an ⲙ one would, according to the rules, expect it
to be changed. The ⲙ in question, however, is the definite
article ⲛ which has been altered because the initial letter of
the noun is an ⲙ .

b)   ⲓ and ⲟⲩ are semi-consonants, and can be treated as vowels or consonants. As a consonant ⲓ is often written ⲉⲓ , and has the phonetic
value 'ɣ'.

c) A quite common tendency is for two similar consonants to be coalesced, e.g. ⲙⲛ̄ⲧⲏ for ⲙⲛ̄ⲧⲧⲏ 'fifteen'.

4 The Vowels (T.§48ff)

Long: ⲓ (or ⲏ), ⲏ , ⲱ (or ⲟⲩ)

Short: ⲁ , ⲉ , ⲟ

When the letter ⲩ appears after ⲉ or ⲁ it is possible that this is an abbreviated writing for ⲉⲟⲩ or ⲁⲟⲩ , exx. ⲛⲉⲩⲛ for ⲛⲉⲟⲩⲛ 'there was'; ⲁⲩⲡⲱⲙⲉ ⲃⲱⲕ for ⲁ-ⲟⲩ-ⲡⲱⲙⲉ ⲃⲱⲕ 'a man went'.

II PRONOUNS

5 A Suffix Pronouns (T.§185ff)

	Forms	Notes on the Forms
S.1	-ⲓ, -ⲧ	Normal ending -ⲓ. If the stem ends in a consonant use -ⲧ. If the stem ends in -ⲧ , no ending: exx. ⲭⲱⲓ 'my head'; ⲡⲁⲧ 'my foot' (for ⲡⲁⲧⲧ̄).
2m.	-ⲕ	
2f.	-ⲉ	Only used when the stem ends in a consonant. If the stem ends in a vowel, no ending; exx. ⲧⲟⲟⲧⲉ 'thy hand'; ⲣⲱ 'thy mouth'
3m.	-ⲩ	
3f.	-ⲥ	
Pl.1	-ⲛ	
2	-ⲧⲛ̄ -ⲧⲏⲩⲧⲛ̄	Before -ⲧⲛ̄ a short vowel is lengthened, e.g. ⲉⲣⲟⲕ 'to thee', but ⲉⲣⲱⲧⲛ̄ 'to you'. When the stem ends in a consonant use -ⲧⲏⲩⲧⲛ̄ .
3	-ⲟⲩ	If the stem ends in ⲁ contraction takes place (see §4 above). After certain verbs the suffix appears as -ⲥⲉ or -ⲥⲟⲩ exx. ⲭⲟⲟⲩ 'to send', ⲧⲛ̄ⲛⲟⲟⲩ 'to send', also the imperatives ⲁⲡⲓ= and ⲁⲛⲓ= (p.45).

6 **Uses**

The suffix pronouns can be attached to:

a) prepositions (p. 51), exx. ⲉⲣⲟⲕ 'to thee'; ⲛ̄ϩⲏⲧϥ̄ 'in it'.

b) verbs, as the object (p. 56), exx. ⲁϥ-ⲕⲁⲁ-ϥ 'he set him';
    ⲁ-ⲥ-ϫⲓⲧϥ̄ 'she took it'. Also, with some verbs, as the subject
    (§53ff).

c) verbal auxiliaries, as the subject (p. 28), exx. ⲁ-ϥ-ⲃⲱⲕ 'he
    went'; ⲛⲉ-ϥ-ϩⲙ̄ⲟⲟⲥ 'he was sitting'.

d) nouns, as possessives; a limited number only, note especially
    ⲉⲓⲁⲧ= 'eye', ⲣⲱ= 'mouth', ⲣⲁⲧ= 'foot', ⲧⲟⲟⲧ= 'hand', ϩⲧⲏ=
    'heart', ϫⲱ= 'head', ϩⲣⲁ= 'face', i.e. ⲣⲱⲕ 'thy mouth',
    ⲧⲟⲟⲧϥ̄ 'his hand' etc.

e) the suffix pronouns can also be used reflexively, e.g. ϥⲛⲁ-ⲙⲟⲣ-ϥ̄
    'he will gird himself' (Besa 50.19)

    Two lines thus ═ after a word indicate that the word in question
    can take a suffix pronoun.

7 B **Independant Pronouns** (T.§197ff)

S.1	ⲁⲛⲟⲕ ⲁⲛϥ-			
2m.	ⲛ̄ⲧⲟⲕ ⲛ̄ⲧⲕ̄-	Pl.1	ⲁⲛⲟⲛ ⲁⲛ (ⲛ̄)-
2f.	ⲛ̄ⲧⲟ ⲛ̄ⲧⲉ-	2	ⲛ̄ⲧⲱⲧⲛ̄ ⲛ̄ⲧⲉⲧⲛ̄-
3m.	ⲛ̄ⲧⲟϥ ⲛ̄ⲧϥ̄-	3	ⲛ̄ⲧⲟⲟⲩ
3f.	ⲛ̄ⲧⲟⲥ		

8 **Uses**

As can be seen from the above table, the 1st, 2nd and 3rd person masculine
singular, as well as the 1st and 2nd persons plural, have both full and
abbreviated forms, known as the Absolute and Construct forms. These can
be used separately or in conjunction as the subject of a non-verbal sentence with nominal predicate (§ 42), and this, indeed, is the only use
for the construct forms. ⲛ̄ⲧϥ̄- occurs but rarely.

Otherwise, the Absolute forms are used to emphasise another word, and
can thus frequently be left untranslated. Very often it is a pronominal

subject in a verbal sentence that is emphasised, exx. ⲁⲛⲟⲕ ⲁⲓϣⲱϫⲉ
'I struggled' (Sh. 42.39.1) ⲉⲓⲍⲙⲟⲟⲥ ⲁⲛⲟⲕ 'while I was sitting'
(Sh. 42.44.18). They can also emphasise a possessive adjective
(12), ⲛⲁⲉⲥⲟⲟⲩ ⲁⲛⲟⲕ 'my sheep' (Sh. 42.59.23); ⲁⲛⲟⲕ ⲧⲁⲙⲁⲁⲩ 'my mother'
(Besa 10.16); an object, ⲁ-ⲧⲉⲩ-ⲁⲅⲁⲡⲏ ⲁⲛⲟⲕ ϫⲓ ⲙ̄ⲙⲟⲓ 'his love reached me'
(Sh. 42.56.1), or even a prepositional phrase, ⲉⲧⲃⲏⲏⲧ ⲁⲛⲟⲕ 'because
of me' (Sh. 42.144.25).

The independent pronouns are also often found preceding a relative construction, exx. ⲛ̄ⲧⲟⲕ ⲡⲉⲛⲧⲁⲕ ϫⲟⲟⲥ 'it is thou who has said' (Sh. 42.84.13)
ⲛ̄ⲧⲱⲧⲛ̄ ⲛⲉⲧⲙⲟⲥⲧⲉ 'it is you who hate' (Sh. 42.91.13), lit. 'you are
those who hate'.

9 C <u>Pronouns of Emphasis or Contrast</u> (T.§§195-196)

The following are employed after a noun or independent pronoun with
emphatic or contrasting meaning. They each take a suffix pronoun,
agreeing in number and gender with the noun or pronoun in question.

a) ⲍⲱⲱ= '(my)self, also, for (my) part'. Note the following forms:
    1st sing. ⲍⲱ(ⲱ), ⲍⲱⲱⲧ ; 2nd sing. fem. ⲍⲱⲱⲧⲉ ; 2nd pl. ⲍⲱⲧⲧⲏⲩⲧⲛ̄ ;
    3rd pl. ⲍⲱⲟⲩ

b) ⲙⲁⲩⲁⲁ(ⲧ)= 'alone, only'

c) ⲟⲩⲁⲁ(ⲧ)= 'alone, only'
    exx. ⲁⲛⲟⲕ ⲍⲱⲱⲧ ⲁⲛ̄ ⲡⲉⲩⲍⲙ̄ϩⲁⲗ 'I also am his servant' (Sh. 42.38.19);
    ϥ̄ϫⲱ ⲇⲉ ⲍⲱⲱⲩ ⲙ̄ⲙⲟⲥ 'he also says' (Sh. 42.54.2); ⲁⲥⲙⲟⲟⲩⲧⲉ̄ ⲙⲁⲩⲁⲁⲥ
    'she has only killed herself' (Sh. 42.97.19); ⲡⲛⲟⲩⲧⲉ ⲙⲁⲩⲁⲁⲩ
    'God alone' (Sh. 42.101.9); ⲣⲁⲕⲟⲧⲉ ⲁⲛ ⲟⲩⲁⲁⲧⲩ̄ 'not only Alexandria'
    (Sh. 42.35.6)

10 D <u>The Possessive Article</u> (T.203)

m. ⲡⲁ- , f. ⲧⲁ- , pl. ⲛⲁ-

This has the literal meaning of 'that/those things belonging to',
though it is often impossible to translate in this manner, exx.
ⲛⲁ ⲡⲡⲁⲗⲗⲁⲧⲟⲛ 'the dwellers in the palace' (Budge, M.T.9.5), lit.

'those belonging to the palace'; ⲛⲁⲧⲡⲟⲗⲓⲥ ⲧⲏⲣⲥ̄ 'all the people of the city' (Budge, M.T. 10.1), lit. 'those belonging to the whole city'; ⲁⲛⲟⲛ ⲛⲁⲡⲉϩⲟⲟⲩ 'we are of the day' (Besa 4.26)

11   E   The Possessive Pronoun (T. § 204)

	Singular		Plural
	Masc.	Fem.	
S.1	ⲡⲱⲓ	ⲧⲱⲓ	ⲛⲟⲩⲓ
2m	ⲡⲱⲕ	ⲧⲱⲕ	ⲛⲟⲩⲕ
2f	ⲡⲱ	ⲧⲱ	ⲛⲟⲩ
3m	ⲡⲱϥ	ⲧⲱϥ	ⲛⲟⲩϥ
3f	ⲡⲱⲥ	ⲧⲱⲥ	ⲛⲟⲩⲥ
Pl.1	ⲡⲱⲛ	ⲧⲱⲛ	ⲛⲟⲩⲛ
2	ⲡⲱⲧⲛ̄	ⲧⲱⲧⲛ̄	ⲛⲟⲩⲧⲛ̄
3	ⲡⲱⲟⲩ	ⲧⲱⲟⲩ	ⲛⲟⲩⲟⲩ

These are used substantively, and stand apart from any other word in the sentence, exx. ⲡⲱⲓ ⲡⲉ ⲡϣⲟϫⲛⲉ 'mine is the counsel' (Pro. 8.14); ⲧⲱⲟⲩ ⲧⲉ ⲧⲙⲛ̄ⲧⲉⲣⲟ ⲛ̄ⲙⲡⲏⲩⲉ 'theirs is the kingdom of heaven' (Mt. 5.10); ⲛⲉⲕϩⲃⲏⲩⲉ ⲛⲉ ⲛⲟⲩϥ 'your works are his' (Besa 23.3); ⲁⲅⲁⲑⲟⲛ ⲛⲓⲙ ⲛⲟⲩϥ ⲛⲉ 'all good things are his' (Sh. 42.72.8)

12   F   The Possessive Adjective (T. § 205)

	Singular		Plural
	Masc.	Fem.	
S.1	ⲡⲁ-	ⲧⲁ-	ⲛⲁ-
2m	ⲡⲉⲕ-	ⲧⲉⲕ-	ⲛⲉⲕ-
2f	ⲡⲟⲩ-	ⲧⲟⲩ-	ⲛⲟⲩ-
3m	ⲡⲉϥ-	ⲧⲉϥ-	ⲛⲉϥ-
3f	ⲡⲉⲥ-	ⲧⲉⲥ-	ⲛⲉⲥ-
Pl.1	ⲡⲉⲛ-	ⲧⲉⲛ-	ⲛⲉⲛ-
2	ⲡⲉⲧⲛ̄-	ⲧⲉⲧⲛ̄-	ⲛⲉⲧⲛ̄-
3	ⲡⲉⲩ-	ⲧⲉⲩ-	ⲛⲉⲩ-
	1	2	3

These possessives are attached to substantives to express 'my', 'thy' etc.

When translating from English into Coptic difficulty is sometimes encountered in deciding which possessive adjective to use. It is best to ask oneself the following questions:

a) is the noun singular or plural?

b) what is the gender of the noun?

Then:

a) if the noun is singular use column 1 for a masculine noun or column 2 for a feminine noun. If the noun is plural use column 3.

b) whichever column is used, move down until the required person is reached.

exx. i) 'his sister'; the noun is singular and feminine, therefore use column 2 and move down to the 3rd person masc. sing. Thus we get Ⲧⲉⳕⲥⲱⲛⲉ

ii) 'her brother'; this time the noun is masculine singular, and so column 1 is employed, and we obtain ⲡⲉⲥⲥⲟⲛ

iii) 'our servants'; the noun is plural, so column 3 is used and we get ⲛⲉⲛ ⳁⲙ̄ⳁⲁⲗ

13 G <u>The Demonstrative Pronoun</u> (T. §§ 201-202)

a) 'This, these'

i) m. ⲡⲁⲓ , f. ⲦⲀⲓ , pl. ⲚⲀⲓ

These are substantives, standing apart from other words, exx. ⲚⲀⲓ ⲦⲎⲣⲟⲩ 'all these things' (Besa 18.27); ⲦⲀⲓ Ⲧⲉ ⲫⲉ 'this is the way' (Sh. 42.163.6)

ii) m. ⲡⲉⲓ-, f. Ⲧⲉⲓ-, pl. Ⲛⲉⲓ-

These can be found in an abbreviated form with the ⲉ omitted. They are always attached to a noun, exx. ⲚⲉⲓⲚⲟ𐤂 ⲚϢⲡⲏⲣⲉ 'these great wonders' (Besa 14.3); ⳁⲙ̄ⲡⲉⲓⲕⲟⲥⲙⲟⲥ 'in this world' (Besa 26.12); Ⲧⲉⲓⲗⲩⲡⲏ 'this grief' (Besa 32.33)

b) 'That, those'

    i) m. ⲡⲏ , f. ⲧⲏ , pl. ⲛⲏ

Used as substantives, exx. ⲛⲏ ⲇⲉ ⲙ̄ⲡⲟⲩⲉⲓⲙⲉ 'but those did not know' (Jo. 10.6); ⲛⲏ ⲇⲉ ⲙ̄ⲡⲟⲩⲧⲁⲁⲥ ⲛⲁⲩ 'but those were not given to them' (Mt. 13.11)

    ii) To render 'that/those man/men' the following construction is employed. The noun is prefixed by the definite article (§18) and followed by the phrase ⲉⲧⲙ̄ⲙⲁⲩ , which literally means 'who/which is there', i.e. ⲡⲣⲱⲙⲉ ⲉⲧⲙ̄ⲙⲁⲩ 'that man'; ⲛ̄ⲣⲱⲙⲉ ⲉⲧⲙ̄ⲙⲁⲩ 'those men'. ⲉⲧⲙ̄ⲙⲁⲩ remains constant, only the article changing depending on whether the noun is singular or plural.

There is a special way of saying 'that which ...' or 'those who ...', see below, p.77.

14 H <u>Interrogative Pronouns</u> See below, § 98

III <u>NOUNS</u>

15 A <u>Gender</u> (T. § 74ff)

There are masculine and feminine nouns. The feminine ending ⲧ̲ , found in the older forms of the language, has completely disappeared in Coptic. Basically, feminine nouns end in ⲉ or a long vowel, masculine nouns in a consonant or a short vowel, exx. ⲥⲟⲛ 'brother'; ⲥⲱⲛⲉ 'sister.

However, there are exceptions to this rule, and the student is strongly urged, especially in the early stages, to check the gender of every noun, however laborious this may be. An example of the dangers of taking things too much for granted is the word for 'beard', ⲙⲟⲣⲧ̄ , which has feminine gender.

A few nouns end with the 3rd person masculine suffix -ⲩ , or the feminine equivalent -ⲥ , thus clearly indicating their gender, exx. ⲥⲟⲟⲩϩⲥ̄ 'congregation'; ⲛⲁϩⲃⲉⲩ 'yoke'.

Greek neuter nouns are treated as masculine in Coptic, e.g. ⲡⲥⲱⲙⲁ 'the body'.

16 B <u>Plural Forms</u>

The majority of nouns have the same form in both singular and plural, the number being indicated by the article. There are, however, a number of nouns possessing special plural forms. For the rules influencing these forms the student is recommended to consult Steindorff, <u>Kurzer abriss der koptischen grammatik</u>, §§ 33-35, and Plumley, <u>Introductory Coptic Grammar</u>, p. 33ff.

Meanwhile, the following list of very common nouns with special plural forms should be studied carefully and, if possible, memorised:

'Woman', sing. ⲥϩⲓⲙⲉ , pl. ϩⲓⲟⲙⲉ ; '<u>Father</u>', sing. ⲉⲓⲱⲧ , pl. ⲉⲓⲟⲧⲉ ; '<u>Thing</u>, <u>work</u>', sing. ϩⲱⲃ , pl. ϩⲃⲏⲩⲉ ; '<u>Temple</u>', sing. ⲣ̄ⲡⲉ , pl. ⲣ̄ⲡⲏⲩⲉ ; '<u>Brother</u>', sing. ⲥⲟⲛ , pl. ⲥⲛⲏⲩ ; '<u>House</u>', sing. ⲏⲓ , pl. ⲏⲟⲩ ; '<u>Lord</u>, <u>master</u>', sing. ⲭⲟⲉⲓⲥ , pl. ⲭⲓⲥⲟⲟⲩⲉ ; '<u>Path</u>, <u>way</u>', sing. ϩⲓⲏ , pl. ϩⲓⲟⲟⲩⲉ ; '<u>Year</u>', sing. ⲣⲟⲙⲡⲉ , pl. ⲣ̄ⲙⲡⲟⲟⲩⲉ ; '<u>Friend</u>, <u>companion</u>', sing. ⲩⲃⲏⲣ , pl. ⲩⲃⲉⲉⲣ ; '<u>Mouth</u>', sing. ⲣⲟ , pl. ⲣⲱⲟⲩ ; '<u>Enemy</u>', sing. ⲭⲁⲭⲉ , pl. ⲭⲓⲭⲉⲉⲩ ; '<u>Head</u>', sing. ⲁⲡⲉ , pl. ⲁⲡⲏⲩⲉ ; '<u>Sky</u>', sing. ⲡⲉ , pl. ⲡⲏⲩⲉ ('heavens'); '<u>Child</u>, <u>son</u>', sing. ⲩⲏⲣⲉ , pl. ⲩⲏⲩ ; '<u>King</u>', sing. ⲣ̄ⲣⲟ , pl. ⲣ̄ⲣⲱⲟⲩ ; '<u>Month</u>', sing. ⲉⲃⲟⲧ , pl. ⲉⲃⲁⲧⲉ .

Greek words do not normally change in the plural. One of those which can is the common word ⲯⲩⲭⲏ 'soul', which sometimes, though not invariably, becomes ⲯⲩⲭⲟⲟⲩⲉ in the plural.

A few dual nouns survive. Note especially ⲟⲩⲉⲣⲏⲧⲉ (f), 'foot', 'feet'; ⲥⲡⲟⲧⲟⲩ 'lip, lips'; ⲥⲛⲁⲩ 'two, fem. ⲥⲛ̄ⲧⲉ . The numeral 2, if it stands before the noun, will take the singular article (§18). The others can take either the singular or plural articles, possessives, etc.

17 C <u>Compound Nouns</u> (T. § 123ff)

Many compound nouns can be formed by attaching prefixes to either nouns or verbs. Below is a list of the commonest prefixes and the meanings they convey. For a complete list consult Till, <u>Koptische grammatik</u>, p. 71ff.

a) ⲙⲁ ⲛ̄- 'place of ...', producing a word expressing a locality, exx.
ⲙⲁ ⲛ̄ⲃⲱⲕ ⲉϩⲟⲩⲛ 'entrance', lit. 'place of going in'; ⲙⲁ ⲛ̄ⲟⲩⲱⲙ
'eating place'; ⲙⲁⲙ̄ⲡⲱⲧ 'place of refuge'

b) ⲣⲙ̄ⲛ̄- 'man of ...' (the ⲛ̄ is not always written), exx. ⲣⲙ̄ⲛ̄ⲕⲏⲙⲉ
'Egyptian'; ⲣⲙ̄ⲛ̄ϯⲙⲉ 'villager', lit. 'man of the village';
ⲣⲙ̄ⲛ̄ⲣⲁⲧ 'footman'. ⲣⲙ̄- is an abbreviation of ⲣⲱⲙⲉ 'man'.

c) ⲙⲛ̄ⲧ- Derived from mdt, 'thing'; it is used to form abstract
<u>feminine</u> nouns, exx. ⲙⲛ̄ⲧⲉⲓⲱⲧ 'fatherhood'; ⲙⲛ̄ⲧϩⲗⲗⲟ 'old age';
ⲙⲛ̄ⲧⲉⲣⲟ 'kingdom'.

d) ⲣⲉϥ- An abbreviation for ⲣⲱⲙⲉ ⲉϥ- '(a) man who ...'; it produces
a word expressing an agent, exx. ⲣⲉϥϣⲁϫⲉ 'speaker'; ⲣⲉϥⲣⲟⲉⲓⲥ
'watchman'; ⲣⲉϥϣⲙ̄ϣⲉ 'worshipper'.

e) ⲁⲧ- 'Not having'; used to produce a negative adjective, exx.
ⲁⲧϣⲁϫⲉ 'speechless'; ⲁⲧⲥⲃⲱ 'ignorant', lit. 'without teaching';
ⲁⲧⲛⲟⲩⲧⲉ 'Godless'.

f) ϭⲓⲛ- 'Act of, manner of'; exx. ϭⲓⲛⲱⲛϩ̄ 'way, means of life';
ϭⲓⲛⲙⲓⲥⲉ 'birth', lit. 'act of giving birth'; ϭⲓⲛⲥⲱⲛⲧ̄ 'creation'.

It is possible for more than one of these prefixes to be found
used in conjunction, exx. ⲙⲛ̄ⲧⲁⲧⲥⲟⲟⲩⲛ 'ignorance'; ⲙⲛ̄ⲧⲣⲉϥϭⲛ̄ⲁⲣⲓⲕⲉ
'fault-finding, criticism'.

When searching for these compounds in the dictionary, look under
the main stem of the word and not under the prefix. Thus, to find
ⲁⲧϣⲁϫⲉ one would look under ϣⲁϫⲉ.

IV THE ARTICLE (T. § 87ff)

18 A The Definite Article
Normally the definite article appears in the form ⲡ- (m), ⲧ- (f),
ⲛ- (pl.) attached to its substantive, exx. ⲡⲣⲱⲙⲉ 'the man',
ⲧⲥⲱⲛⲉ 'the sister', ⲛ̄ⲣⲱⲙⲉ 'the men'.

19 On the following occasions, however, it assumes the fuller form
ⲡⲉ- (m), ⲧⲉ- (f), ⲛⲉ- (pl.):

a) before certain substantives that are expressions of time, Ⲧⲉⲣⲟⲙⲡⲉ 'the year'; ⲡⲉⳉⲟⲟⲩ 'the day'; Ⲧⲉⲩⲛⲟⲩ 'the hour', (for Ⲧⲉⲟⲩⲛⲟⲩ , see §4); ⲦⲉⲩϢⲏ 'the night' (for ⲦⲉⲟⲩϢⲏ).

b) before a substantive beginning with two consonants or a consonant followed by a semi-consonant (see §3b), exx Ⲧⲉⳡⲓⲙⲉ 'the woman'; ⲚⲉⳒⲠⲏⲣⲉ 'the wonders'; ⲡⲉⳒⲂⲏⲣ 'the friend'; Ⲧⲉⳉⲓⲏ 'the way'; ⲡⲉⳉⲟⲩⲟ 'the greater part'.

20 Sometimes, however, one of the two initial consonants is sonant (see p.2). On these occasions the Copts themselves are by no means consistent. Thus the noun ⲣ̄ⲡⲉ , 'temple', can be found preceded by either form of the article. A good example can be found in Sh. 73.9.27 and note 11 where two versions of the same ms. have differing forms of the article before ⲣ̄ⲡⲉ. On the other hand, words like ⲣ̄ⲣⲟ, 'king', and ⳉ̄ⲗⲟ , 'old man', consistently take the shorter form ⲡ- . While the reasons for this apparent contradiction may be etymological, it is impossible to propose a set of rules to act as a guide in these circumstances. The examples given in Crum's dictionary or in Wilmet's Concordance du nouveau testament Sahidique will give an indication as to what form of the article is permitted.

Compound nouns beginning with ⲘⲚ̄Ⲧ- or ⲣ̄Ⲙ- take the shorter form of the article.

21 The Greek letters ⲑ , ⲫ , ⲭ and ⲯ , as well as Greek words beginning ⳉⲣ- in Coptic, are treated as double consonants, and therefore take the full form of the article, exx. Ⲧⲉⲯⲩⲭⲏ 'the soul'; Ⲧⲉⲭⲱⲣⲁ 'the land'; ⲡⲉⳉⲣⲁⲃⲃⲉⲓ 'the Master'.

22 Apart from its normal usage, there are occasions in Coptic when the definite article is used even though it would not be expressed in English:

a) normally, before foreign place-names, exx. Ⲧⲥⲁⲙⲁⲣⲓⲁ 'Samaria'; ⲦⲂⲁⲃⲩⲗⲟⲛ 'Babylon'; ϯⲗⲟⲩⲙⲁⲓⲁ 'Edom'; ⲡⲓⲏ̄ⲗ 'Israel' (abbreviation for ⲡⲓⲥⲣⲁⲏⲗ).

b) before the words 'God' and 'Christ' – ⲡⲛⲟⲩⲧⲉ , ⲡⲉⲭⲥ̄ (for ⲡⲉⲭⲣⲓⲥⲧⲟⲥ)

c) before a noun, acting as a vocative, e.g. ⲡⲭⲟⲉⲓⲥ 'O Lord'.

Some words are often treated as plural which in English would not be understood in this way, exx. ⲙⲟⲟⲩ 'water', which will often be found preceded by the plural article (ⲛ̄ⲙⲟⲟⲩ), and similarly ⲥⲁⲣⲝ 'flesh' (ⲛ̄ⲥⲁⲣⲝ) and ⲟⲉⲓⲕ 'bread' (ⲛ̄ⲟⲉⲓⲕ).

23 B The Indefinite Article

Masc. and fem. sing. ⲟⲩ- , pl. ϩⲉⲛ-

Attached directly to the substantive, exx. ⲟⲩⲣⲱⲙⲉ 'a man', ϩⲉⲛⲣⲱⲙⲉ 'men' or 'some men'.

24 Apart from its normal usage, the indefinite article is also employed:

a) with abstract nouns, exx ⲟⲩⲙ̄ⲕⲁϩ 'grief'; ⲟⲩⲙⲟⲥⲧⲉ 'hatred'; ⲟⲩϣⲡⲏⲣⲉ 'amazement'; ⲟⲩⲁⲅⲁⲑⲟⲛ ⲛⲁⲛ ⲡⲉ 'it is good for us' (Sh. 42.181.8)

b) with nouns of material, exx. ⲟⲩⲛⲟⲩⲃ ⲙⲛ̄ ⲟⲩϩⲁⲧ 'gold and silver' (Besa 2.11); ⲟⲩⲥⲟⲣⲧ̄ 'wool'

c) in adverbial expressions with the preposition ϩⲛ̄- 'in', e.g. ϩⲛ̄ⲟⲩϣⲱⲡ 'suddenly', lit. 'in a moment' (see § 81b).

The singular indefinite article is often contracted if it follows ⲁ or ⲉ , see § 4.

V THE GENITIVE (T. § 111ff)

25 Normally, the two elements forming the genitival expression are linked by ⲛ̄ (ⲙ̄ before ⲙ̄ and ⲡ , see § 3a), exx. ⲡⲉⲥⲡⲉⲣⲙⲁ ⲛ̄ⲛⲉⲛⲉⲓⲟⲧⲉ 'the seed of our fathers' (Sh. 42.182.1); ⲛ̄ⲥⲟⲣⲥ̄ ⲙ̄ⲡⲇⲓⲁⲃⲟⲗⲟⲥ 'the snares of the Devil' (Sh. 42.161.29); ⲛ̄ⲥⲁⲣⲝ ⲛ̄ⲛⲉⲩⲥⲱⲙⲁ 'the flesh of their bodies' (Sh. 42.162.12)

26 However, ⲛ̄ⲧⲉ- (ⲛ̄ⲧⲁ= before suffixes) is used instead of ⲛ̄ :

a) when the preceding noun is prefixed by the indefinite article or demonstrative pronoun, exx. ⲡⲉⲓϣⲏⲣⲉ ⲛ̄ⲧⲉ ⲡⲣⲱⲙⲉ 'this son of man' (Jo. 12.34); ⲟⲩϩⲱⲃ ⲛ̄ⲧⲉ ⲡⲇⲓⲁⲃⲟⲗⲟⲥ 'a scheme of the Devil' (St. A. 16.34); ⲟⲩⲙⲛ̄ⲧⲉⲣⲟ ⲛ̄ⲧⲉ ⲙ̄ⲡⲏⲩⲉ 'a kingdom of the heavens' (Sh. 73.30.8)

b) Usually if the preceding noun is <u>treated</u> as undefined, even though the indefinite article is not written, e.g. ⲉⲧⲣⲉⲩ ϣⲱⲡⲉ ⲛ̄ϣⲏⲣⲉ ⲛ̄ⲧⲉ ⲡⲛⲟⲩⲧⲉ 'that they might be sons of God' (Jo. 1.12)

c) when the preceding noun is qualified by an adjective or similar construction, though not when it is qualified by a numeral, exx. ⲟⲩⲛⲟϭ ⲛ̄ⲁⲅⲓⲟⲥ ⲛ̄ⲧⲉⲡⲛⲟⲩⲧⲉ 'a great saint of God' (Budge, Martyrdoms 212.32); ϩⲁϩ ⲛ̄ϣⲏⲣⲉ ⲛ̄ⲧⲉ ⲡⲛⲟⲩⲧⲉ 'many sons of God' (Sh. 73.31.23)

Occasionally this rule is not applied, e.g. ⲡϩⲁⲡ ⲙ̄ⲙⲉ ⲙ̄ⲡⲛⲟⲩⲧⲉ 'the righteous judgement of God' (Besa 46.3)

When the adjective ⲧⲏⲣ= 'all' qualifies a substantive the genitive takes the shorter form ⲛ̄ , e.g. ϩⲉⲛⲕⲉϩⲃⲏⲩⲉ ⲧⲏⲣⲟⲩ ⲛ̄ⲇⲓⲕⲁⲓⲟⲥⲩⲛⲏ 'all other works of righteousness' (Sh. 73.30.28)

d) sometimes ⲛ̄ⲧⲉ is employed between two proper names, but this rule is not consistent, exx. ⲃⲏⲑⲗⲉⲉⲙ ⲛ̄ⲧⲉ ϯⲟⲩⲇⲁⲓⲁ 'Bethlehem of Judaea', but ⲧⲕⲁⲛⲁ ⲛ̄ⲧⲅⲁⲗⲓⲗⲁⲓⲁ 'Cana of Galilee'.

VI THE ADJECTIVE (T. § 114ff)

27 A few adjectives stand immediately after the noun. Note especially ⲛⲓⲙ 'all, every'; ϣⲏⲙ 'little, young'; ⲧⲏⲣ= (+ suffixes) 'all', exx. ⲛ̄ⲕⲁ ⲛⲓⲙ 'all things' (Jo. 1.3); ⲡⲧⲟⲟⲩ ϣⲏⲙ 'the little mountain' (Ps. 41.6); ⲡⲉⲟⲟⲩ ⲧⲏⲣϥ̄ 'all the glory' (Ps. 44.13).

28 Normally, however, the adjective is linked to its noun by ⲛ̄ (ⲙ̄ before ⲙ or ⲡ). Some adjectives, of which ⲛⲟϭ, 'great' and ϩⲁϩ , 'many', are by far the commonest, precede the noun, but usually the adjective follows, exx. ϩⲉⲛⲛⲟϭ ⲛ̄ⲱⲛⲉ 'some great stones' (Sh. 42.162.10); ϩⲁϩ ⲛ̄ⲥⲟⲡ 'many times' (Sh. 42.114.23); ⲛ̄ⲣⲱⲙⲉ ⲛ̄ⲁⲧⲥⲃⲱ 'the ignorant men' (Sh. 42.180.8); ⲧⲉϩⲣⲱ ⲛ̄ⲥⲁⲧⲉ 'the fiery furnace' (Besa 65.34); ⲡϩⲁⲡ ⲙ̄ⲙⲉ 'the just judgement' (Besa 68.23).

29 A relative clause can be used adjectivally (p.73ff), exx. ⲡⲣⲁⲛ ⲉⲧⲟⲩⲁⲁⲃ ⲙ̄ⲡⲛⲟⲩⲧⲉ ⲉⲧⲥⲙⲁⲙⲁⲁⲧ 'the holy name of the blessed God' (Sh. 42.17.17); ⲡϣⲁϫⲉ ⲉⲧⲥⲏϩ 'the written word', lit. 'the word which is written' (Sh. 42.175.9).

30   So can the Present Circumstantial tense (§76) functioning as a relative, exx. ογαrrελoc εчογλλβ 'a holy angel' (Sh. 42.40.15); ζωβ ΝΙΜ
εчζooγ 'every evil thing' (Sh. 42.161.11); ογπνλ εчϫoce Ν̄ζΗτ   'an
exalted spirit' (Sh. 42.162.3).

A few adjectives have masculine and feminine forms, e.g. 'wise' –
cλβε (m), cλβΗ (f).

31   The word κε-, 'other', (pl. ζενκε-) has the following possible uses:

   a)   attached to a noun, exx. ζενκερ̄ρωoγ 'other kings' (Sh. 42.68.16);
       κεεγλrreλιoΝ 'another gospel' (Besa 79.25); κεμλθΗτΗc   'another
       disciple' (Jo. 18.15).

   b)   used substantively, either in the form κεoγλ, when it can be pre-
       ceded by the definite article ('the other') or demonstrative pro-
       noun ('this other'), or in the form ζενκooγε 'others', Ν̄κooγε
       'the others'.

   c)   preceded by the definite article or a possessive, and itself
       attached to a noun, giving the meaning 'also, even', exx. πκεπετρoc
       'Peter also' (Acts 12.3); Νετν̄κεειoτε   'your fathers also' (Besa
       55.29).

VII   <u>NUMERALS</u> (T. §156ff)

32   A   <u>Cardinals</u>

     a)   1 – 9

		Absolute		Construct	With Tens
		Masc.	Fem.		
1		ογλ	ογει		-ογε (m) -ογει (f)
2		cΝαγ	cΝ̄τε		– cν̄ooγc (m)
					– cν̄ooγce (f)
3		ϣoμν̄τ	ϣoμτε	ϣμ̄τ-, ϣμν̄τ-	– ϣoμτε
4		ϥ̄τooγ	ϥ̄τo (ε)	ϥ̄τoγ -, ϥ̄τεγ-	– λγτε
5		†ογ	†ε		– τΗ
6		cooγ	co (ε)	cεγ-	– λcε
7		cλϣϥ̄	cλϣϥε		– cλϣϥ (ε)
8		ϣμoγΝ	ϣμoγΝε		– ϣμΗΝ (ε)
9		ψιc, ψιτ	ψιτε		

14

b) 10 - 90

  10 ⲙⲏⲧ (m), ⲙⲏⲧⲉ (f), ⲙⲛ̄ⲧ- (construct)

  20 ϫⲟⲩⲱⲧ (m), ϫⲟⲩⲱⲧⲉ (f), ϫⲟⲩⲧ- (construct)

  30 ⲙⲁⲁⲃ (m) ⲙⲁⲁⲃⲉ (f) ⲙⲁⲃ- (construct)

  40 ϩⲙⲉ : 50 ⲧⲁⲓⲟⲩ : 60 ⲥⲉ :

  70 ϣϥⲉ (also written ϣⲃⲉ, ⲥⲯ̄ϥⲉ)

  80 ϩⲙⲉⲛⲉ , ϩⲙ(ⲉ)ⲛⲉ-(construct)

  90 ⲡⲥ̄ⲧⲁⲓⲟⲩ , ⲯⲁⲓⲧ- (construct)

c) 11 - 99

The ten unit is attached directly to the second element (1-9): Where construct forms of the tens exist they are normally used, but the construct form of 30 is not invariably employed. If the second element is 4 or 6 (-ⲁϥⲧⲉ or -ⲁⲥⲉ) a ⲧ is inserted between the two elements: exx. ⲙⲛ̄ⲧϣⲙⲏⲛ '18' ⲧⲁⲓⲟⲩⲥⲁϣϥ̄ '57'; ⲙⲛ̄ⲧⲁⲥⲉ 'sixteen'; ⲙⲁⲁⲃⲉ ϣⲙⲏⲛⲉ ⲛ̄ⲣⲟⲙⲡⲉ '38 years' (Jo. 5.5); ⲥⲉⲧⲁⲥⲉ '66'

d) 100 ϣⲉ ; 200 ϣⲏⲧ

e) 300 - 900

Two possible constructions:

  i) the construct form of the unit (only possible with 3, 4 and
      6) + ϣⲉ , e.g. ϣⲙⲛ̄ⲧ ⲛ̄ϣⲉ '300'

  ii) the absolute form of the unit (i.e. numbers 3-9) + ⲛ̄ϣⲉ ,
      exx. ϣⲙⲟⲩⲛ ⲛ̄ϣⲉ '800'; ⲥⲁϣϥ̄ ⲛ̄ϩⲉ '700', etc.

f) 1,000 ϣⲟ

g) 2,000 - 9,000

Similar constructions to e) above, ϣⲉ being replaced by ϣⲟ ; note ϭⲓⲥⲧⲃⲁ, '5,000', lit. 'half 10,000', exx. ⲥⲉⲩϣⲟ or ⲥⲟⲟⲩⲛ̄ϣⲟ '6,000'; ϣⲙⲟⲩⲛ ⲛ̄ϣⲟ '8,000', etc.

h) 10,000 ⲧⲃⲁ

33 B   <u>Syntax of the Cardinals</u>

   a) The most common construction is NUMERAL – N̄ – NOUN, exx. ⲥⲁϣϥ̄
      ⲛ̄ⲟⲉⲓⲕ 'seven loaves' (Sh. 42.72.11); ϩⲙⲉ ⲛ̄ⲣⲟⲙⲡⲉ 'forty
      years' (Ps. 94.10); ⲥⲟⲟⲩ ⲛ̄ϩⲱⲃ 'six things' (Besa 47.3); ⲭⲟⲩⲱⲧ
      ⲛ̄ϣⲟ ⲛ̄ⲣⲱⲙⲉ   '20,000 men' (Sh. 42.69.9); ϣⲟⲙⲛ̄ⲧ ⲛ̄ⲉⲃⲟⲧ
      'three months' (Sh. 42.69.11)

   b) but the numeral 2 normally <u>follows</u> the noun with no particle
      intervening, i.e. ⲡⲣⲱⲙⲉ ⲥⲛⲁⲩ 'the two men'; ⲧⲉⲥϩⲓⲙⲉ ⲥⲛ̄ⲧⲉ 'the
      two women', etc.

34 The numeral agrees in gender with the noun, WHICH IS ALWAYS TREATED
   AS SINGULAR, i.e. when the noun is qualified by the definite article,
   possessive adjective or demonstrative pronoun, the SINGULAR forms are
   employed, exx. ⲡⲥⲁϣϥ̄ ⲛ̄ϣⲏⲣⲉ ϣⲏⲙ 'the seven young men' (C.L. 32.1);
   ⲧϯⲉ ⲙ̄ⲡⲁⲣⲑⲉⲛⲟⲥ ⲛ̄ⲥⲁⲃⲏ 'the five wise virgins (Besa 50.22); ϣⲟⲙⲛ̄ⲧ ⲛ̄ϩⲟⲟⲩ
   ⲙⲛ̄ ϣⲟⲙⲧⲉ ⲛ̄ⲟⲩϣⲏ   'three days and three nights' (Cha. 42.25)

35 Composite numbers can be constructed:

   a) by direct juxtaposition of the two elements, exx. ϣⲉ ⲧⲁⲓⲟⲩ ⲛ ⲝⲉⲥⲧⲏⲥ
      ⲛ̄ⲛⲉϩ '150 measures of oil' (Sh. 42.70.3); ϣⲉ ⲭⲟⲩⲧϣⲙⲏⲛ ⲛ̄ⲣⲱⲙⲉ
      '128 men' (Besa 42.12)

   b) by inserting ⲙⲛ̄ , 'and', between the elements, exx. ⲧⲁⲓⲟⲩ ⲙⲛ̄
      ϩⲙⲉⲧⲁϥⲧⲉ ⲛ̄ⲣⲱⲙⲉ '94 men' (50 + 44) (Sh. 42.69.16) ⲧⲁⲓⲟⲩ
      ⲙⲛ̄ⲥⲛⲁⲩ '52' (Sh. 42.69.18); ⲧⲁⲓⲟⲩ ⲙⲛ̄ⲥⲁϣϥ̄ ⲛ̄ϣⲉ ⲙⲛ̄ ⲥⲟⲟⲩ ⲛ̄ⲧⲃⲁ ⲛ̄ϩⲟⲙⲛ̄ⲧ
      '60,750 copper coins' (50 + 700 + 60,000) (Sh. 42.71.7)

36 C <u>Ordinals</u>
    ⲙⲉϩ- is placed before the cardinal, exx. ⲙⲉϩϥ̄ⲧⲟⲟⲩ 'fourth';
    ⲙⲉϩⲙⲁⲁⲃ 'thirtieth'. Note ϣⲟⲣⲡ̄, 'first', ϣⲣ̄ⲡ- before nouns.
    Used adverbially it takes the form ⲛ̄ϣⲟⲣⲡ̄.

37 There are two possible constructions:

   a) ORDINAL – N̄ – NOUN exx. ⲧⲙⲉϩⲥⲟⲉ ⲛ̄ⲣⲟⲙⲡⲉ 'the 6th year (Besa 41.27);
      ϩⲙ̄ⲡⲙⲉϩⲥⲁϣϥ̄ ⲛ̄ⲉⲃⲟⲧ ⲛ̄ⲥⲟⲩⲙⲛ̄ⲧⲥⲛⲟⲟⲩⲥ ⲙ̄ⲡⲉⲃⲟⲧ 'in the 7th month, on the
      12th day of the month' (Besa 41.28) (See below, § 38).

b) NOUN — N̄ — ORDINAL   Not common in Sahidic

ⲙⲉϩⲥⲛⲁⲩ , 'second', usually stands before the noun, e.g.
ⲧⲙⲉϩⲥⲛ̄ⲧⲉ ⲛ̄ⲟⲩⲣ̄ϣⲉ 'the 2nd watch' (Besa 50.20). Very occasionally,
however, a different construction is used, with ⲙⲉϩ- prefixed directly to the noun and ⲥⲛⲁⲩ or ⲥⲛ̄ⲧⲉ following the noun, e.g.
ⲧⲙⲉϩⲣⲟⲙⲡⲉ ⲛ̄ⲥⲛ̄ⲧⲉ 'the 2nd year' (Till 293.28).

38 When the day of a month or a festival is indicated the <u>cardinal</u> number
is used instead of the ordinal, exx. ⲛ̄ⲥⲟⲩ ⲙⲛ̄ⲧⲁⲩⲧⲉ ⲙ̄ⲡⲉⲃⲟⲧ ⲡⲁϣⲟⲛⲥ̄
'on the 14th day of the month Pashone' (Till 288.10); ⲛ̄ⲥⲟⲩ ⲥⲁϣϥ̄ ⲙ̄ⲡⲉⲃⲟⲧ
ⲉⲡⲏⲫ 'on the 7th day of the month Epeph' (Besa 126.8)

Note also the use of the word ⲥⲟⲩ for 'day' rather than the more common
ϩⲟⲟⲩ . This is normal practice with dates.

39 For a discussion of the Coptic calendar and their method of dating see
Till, <u>op. cit.,</u> § 176 ff.

40 The Greek method, whereby the letters of the alphabet had numerical
value, is employed but rarely in Sahidic, and then only in dates.

VIII   <u>NON-VERBAL SENTENCES</u>   (T. § 242ff)

41 These are sentences which do not contain a finite verb, this being
replaced by 'is' or 'are', referred to in grammars as the COPULA.
The copula is sometimes not expressed in Coptic, (see below), but
normally it appears in the form ⲡⲉ (m), ⲧⲉ (f) or ⲛⲉ (pl).

The <u>subject</u> in these sentences can be a noun or pronoun. The
<u>predicate</u> can be a noun, pronoun or adverb.

Two types of non-verbal sentence can be distinguished:
A   Those with nominal predicate
B   Those with adverbial predicate

42 A <u>Non-Verbal Sentences with Nominal Predicate</u>
a) <u>with a pronominal subject</u>
     i) 1st and 2nd persons, singular and plural; direct juxtaposition,
         SUBJECT PRECEDING THE PREDICATE. The independent pronouns (§7)

17

are employed, either in the absolute or construct form. Sometimes both are used for emphasis, the absolute then preceding, exx. ⲁⲛⲟⲕ ⲟⲩϨⲏⲕⲉ ⲁⲛ︦ϥ ⲟⲩⲉⲃⲓⲏⲛ 'I am a poor man, I am a miserable man' (Besa 91.3); ⲁⲛⲟⲛ ⲛⲉϥϣⲏⲣⲉ 'we are his sons' (Besa 30.2); ⲁⲛⲟⲕ ⲇⲉ ⲁⲛ︦ϥ ⲟⲩⲣⲉϥ︦ⲣⲛⲟⲃⲉ 'But I am a sinner' (Sh. 42.118.6); ⲛ︦ⲧ︦ⲕ ⲟⲩⲣⲱⲙⲉ ⲛ︦ⲥⲛⲟϥ 'you are a bloody man' (Besa 22.14)

The copula can sometimes intrude into this construction, when it usually takes the form ⲡⲉ, exx. ⲁⲛⲟⲕ ⲡⲉ ⲡⲛⲟⲩⲧⲉ 'I am God' (Sh. 42.84.14); ⲁⲛⲟⲕ ⲡⲉ ⲡⲣⲟ 'I am the door' (Jo. 10.36).

ii) 3rd person singular and plural; the above construction – independent pronoun + predicate – can also be found with the 3rd person, when the pronoun will, with very rare exceptions, take the full form, exx. ⲛ︦ⲧⲟϥ ⲡⲉ ⲡ︦ⲣⲣⲟ ⲙ︦ⲡⲉⲟⲟⲩ 'he is the king of glory' (Ps. 23.10); ⲛ︦ⲧⲟϥ ⲡⲉ ⲡⲉⲛⲛⲟⲩⲧⲉ 'he is our God' (Ps. 94.7); ⲛ︦ⲧⲟⲥ ⲡⲉ ⲡⲱⲛϨ ⲙ︦ⲡⲧⲏⲣϥ︦ 'she is the life of mankind' (Sh. 73.15.20).

But normally in a sentence of this pattern, i.e. 'he/she/it/ they is/are ...' THE PREDICATE PRECEDES THE COPULA REPRESENTING THE SUBJECT, exx. ⲡⲉϥⲁⲅⲅⲉⲗⲟⲥ ⲡⲉ 'it is his angel' (Acts 12.15); ⲛⲉⲕϣⲃⲏⲣ ⲛⲉ 'they are thy friends' (Sh. 42.32.22); Ϩⲉⲛⲙⲁⲓⲡⲁⲑⲟⲥ ⲛⲉ 'they are sensualists' (Besa 119.17)
The copula agrees in number and gender with the predicate.

43 b) with a nominal subject, i.e. 'A is B', where both A and B are nouns. The elements subject, predicate and copula can be arranged in the following three ways:

i) PREDICATE   COPULA   SUBJECT
exx. ⲡϨⲁⲃⲥ̄ ⲛ̄ⲛⲁⲟⲩⲉⲣⲏⲧⲉ ⲡⲉ ⲡⲉⲕϣⲁϫⲉ 'Your word is the lamp of my feet' (Besa 74.5); ⲟⲩⲣⲉϥ︦ⲣⲟⲩⲟⲉⲓⲛ ⲅⲁⲣ ⲧⲉ ⲧⲉⲛⲧⲟⲗⲏ ⲉⲧⲛⲁⲛⲟⲩⲥ 'For the good commandment is a lamp' (Besa 74.4); ⲑⲓⲗⲏⲙ ⲛ̄ⲧⲡⲉ ⲧⲉ ⲧⲉⲧⲛ̄Ϩⲉⲛⲉⲉⲧⲏ 'your convent is the heavenly Jerusalem' (Besa 106.17)

18

ii) SUBJECT   COPULA   PREDICATE

exx. ⲦⲤⲱϣⲉ ⲡⲉ ⲡⲕⲟⲥⲙⲟⲥ   'the field is the world. (Mt. 13.38); ⲡⲟⲉⲓⲕ ⲅⲁⲣ ⲡⲉ ⲡϣⲏⲣⲉ ⲙ̄ⲡⲛⲟⲩⲧⲉ 'for the bread is the Son of God' (Jo. 6.33); ⲛ̄ⲭⲁⲓⲟ︤ⲍ̄ ⲇⲉ ⲛⲉ ⲛ̄ⲁⲅⲅⲉⲗⲟⲥ   'but the reapers are the angels' (Mt. 13.39)

This construction seems to be often employed when there is a desire to retain the word order of the Greek original. It is also the order normally, though not invariably, used when the subject is a demonstrative pronoun, exx. ⲛⲁⲓ ⲛⲉ ⲛⲉⲌⲟⲟⲩ ⲙ̄ⲡⲭⲓⲕⲃⲁ 'these are the days of retribution' (Sh. 73.15.8); ⲡⲁⲓ ⲡⲉ ⲡⲟⲩⲱϣ ⲙ̄ⲡⲛⲟⲩⲧⲉ   'this is the wish of God' (Besa 35.4)

iii) SUBJECT   PREDICATE   COPULA

exx. ⲡⲙⲁ ⲟⲩⲭⲁⲓⲉ ⲡⲉ   'the place is a desert' (Mt. 14.15); ⲡⲛⲟⲩⲧⲉ ⲟⲩⲡ̄ⲛ̄ⲁ̄ ⲡⲉ 'God is a spirit' (Besa 17.31); ⲡⲗⲁⲥ Ⲍⲱⲱϥ ⲟⲩⲕⲱ︤Ⲍ̄Ⲧ̄ ⲡⲉ   'the tongue also is a fire' (Besa 98.5); ⲡⲟⲩⲉⲓⲱⲧ ⲟⲩⲁⲙⲟⲣⲣⲁⲓⲟⲥ ⲡⲉ ⲁⲩⲱ ⲧⲟⲩⲙⲁⲁⲩ ⲟⲩⲭⲉⲧⲧⲁⲓⲁ ⲧⲉ   'your father is an Amorite and your mother is a Hittite' (Besa 109.17); ⲡⲉⲓⲙⲁ ⲅⲁⲣ ⲡⲏⲓ ⲙ̄ⲡⲛⲟⲩⲧⲉ ⲡⲉ   'for this place is the house of God' (Besa 26.23).

When this construction is used there is often emphasis on the subject.

In non-verbal sentences with nominal predicate the past tense is expressed by placing ⲛⲉ at the head of the sentence, e.g. ⲛⲉ Ⲍⲉⲛⲟⲩⲱ︤Ⲍ︦ⲉ ⲅⲁⲣ ⲛⲉ 'for they were fishermen' (Mt. 4.18).

44   Whichever order is used, whenever the subject and predicate agree in number and gender so will the copula. When they do not agree use ⲡⲉ. For a detailed discussion of concord in non-verbal sentences see M. Chaine, La proposition nominale dans les dialectes coptes, p. 33ff.

45 B <u>Non-Verbal Sentences with Adverbial Predicate</u>

The predicate can be an adverb or an adverbial expression, (i.e. 'the man is <u>outside</u>' or 'the man is <u>in the house</u>').

The subject can be nominal or pronominal. In either case THE SUBJECT DIRECTLY PRECEDES THE ADVERBIAL PREDICATE. For present meaning the prefixes of the 1st Present (§58), 2nd Present (§74) or Circumstantial (§76) tenses are employed, the latter two being identical in form. When the 1st Present is used and the subject is nominal, the fact that this tense has no nominal prefix means that the subject and predicate stand alone; exx. ⲠⲈⲬⲤ ⲘⲠⲈⲒⲘⲀ 'Christ is here' (Mt. 24.23) (1st Present); ⲈⲢⲈ ⲠⲘⲞⲨ ⲘⲚ ⲠⲰⲚⲎ ⳍⲚⲦⲞⲒⲤ ⲘⲠⲖⲀⲤ 'in the power of the tongue are death and life' (Besa 85.23) (2nd Present); ⲈⲢⲈⳍⲈⲚⲢⲈⲨ ⲯⲀⲀⲢ ⳍⲒⲰⲞⲨ 'demons being in them' (Mt. 8.28) (Circumstantial); ⳚⳍⲒ ⲠⲬⲀⲈⲒⲈ 'he is in the desert' (Mt. 24.26) (1st Present).

When the subject is undefined, ('a man', 'some men' or simply 'men'), it <u>must</u> be preceded by the impersonal verbs ⲞⲨⲚ- 'there is' or (Ⲙ̅)ⲘⲚ̅- 'there is not' (§54), e.g. ⲞⲨⲚ ⲞⲨⲆⲀⲒⲘⲞⲚⲒⲞⲚ ⳍⲒⲰⲰⳤ 'a demon is in him' (Mt. 11.18).

To achieve past meaning in a sentence with adverbial predicate the prefixes of the Imperfect tense (§60) are used, exx. ⲚⲈⲒⳍⲘ̅-ⲠⲈⲨⲦⲈⲔⲞ ⲠⲈ 'I was in the prison' (Mt. 25.36); ⲚⲈⲨⳍⲘ̅-ⲠⲔⲞⲤⲘⲞⲤ ⲠⲈ 'he was in the world' (Jo. 1.10); ⲚⲈⲤⲘ̅ⲘⲀⲨ 'she was there' (Mt. 27.61).

Note the presence in two of the above examples of the element ⲠⲈ. This is quite common in sentences of this type, as it is in verbal sentences employing the Imperfect tense (§ 60).

46   There is no method in Coptic for expressing futurity in non-verbal sentences. The idea of future existence is conveyed by the verb ⲯⲰⲠⲈ (Qual. ⲯⲞⲞⲠ, §51), prefixed by one of the Future tenses (§62 ff), exx. ⲠⲈⲔⲢ̅ⲠⲘⲈⲈⲨⲈ ⲚⲀⲯⲰⲠⲈ 'thy memorial shall be' (Besa 126.26); ⲠⲈⲦⲚ̅ⲤⲚⲞⳤ ⲈⳤⲈⲯⲰⲠⲈ ⲈⳍⲢⲀⲒ ⲈⲬⲰⲦⲚ̅ 'your blood shall be upon you' (Besa 117.21).

47   To negate a non-verbal sentence N̄ .... ⲁⲛ is used, though
the N̄ is often omitted, exx. ⲙ̄ⲡⲁϩⲁⲓ ⲅⲁⲣ ϩⲙ̄ⲡⲁϩⲓ ⲁⲛ 'for my
husband is not in my house' (Pro. 7.19); ⲛⲉ ⲡⲉⲧⲙ̄ⲙⲁⲩ ⲁⲛ ⲡⲟⲩⲟⲉⲓⲛ
'that one was not the light' (Jo. 1.8); ⲙ̄ⲡⲥⲟⲡ ⲁⲛ ⲡⲉ 'it is not
the time' (Sh. 73.13.8); ⲟⲩⲙⲟⲉⲓϩⲉ ⲁⲛ ⲧⲉ 'it is not a wonder'
(Sh. 73.22.3); N̄ⲁⲛⲟⲕ ⲁⲛ 'it is not I' (St. A. 9.4).

48   <u>Conclusion</u>

The non-verbal sentence often proves to be one of the most confus-
ing aspects of Coptic grammar for the beginner. In a work of this
nature, with its attempt to simplify what is frequently not simple,
the treatment is bound to be rather superficial. There will be
occasions when the 'rules' listed above do not seem to apply.
Rather than blame the Copts for inconsistency we should assume
that our knowledge is still imperfect. Apart from the more comprehensive grammars there are several studies devoted specifically
to the problems of non-verbal sentences:

J. Vergote, 'La phrase nominale en copte', in <u>Coptic Studies in
Honour of Walter Ewing Crum</u>, p. 229ff.

M. Chaine, <u>La proposition nominale dans les dialectes coptes</u> (1955)

J. Polotsky, 'Nominalsatz und cleft sentence in koptischen', in
<u>Orientalia</u>, Vol. 21 (1962), p.413 ff.

W. Till, 'Die satzarten im koptischen', in <u>Mitteilungen des
Instituts fur Orientforschung</u>, Band 11, Heft 3 (1954), p. 378 ff.

<u>EXERCISE 1</u>

This exercise is principally concerned with non-verbal sentences,
but the opportunity has been taken to include examples which also
test the student on earlier sections of the grammar. Underlining
indicates emphasis.

Vocabulary

ⲁⲅⲁⲑⲟⲛ	Good thing (m)	ⲥⲱ	Drink (verb or m. noun)
ⲁⲃⲣⲁϩⲁⲙ	Abraham	ⲥⲃⲱ	Teaching, doctrine (f)
ⲉⲃⲟⲗ	Out; + ϩⲛ- (or ⲛϩⲏⲧ⸗)	ⲥⲁⲃⲃⲁⲧⲟⲛ	Sabbath (m)
	Out of, from (Crum 34a ff)	ⲥⲙⲏ	Voice (f)
ⲉⲥⲟⲟⲩ	Sheep (m)	ⲥⲟⲟⲛⲉ	Robber (m)
ⲇⲓⲁⲃⲟⲗⲟⲥ	Devil (m)	ⲥⲛⲟϥ	Blood (m)
ⲓⲟⲩⲇⲁⲓ	Jew (m)	ⲥⲡⲉⲣⲙⲁ	Seed (m)
ⲓ̅ⲥ̅	Jesus, for ⲓⲏⲥⲟⲩⲥ	ⲥⲁⲣⲝ	Flesh (f)
ⲕⲁϩ	Earth, land (m)	ⲥⲱⲧⲡ	Chosen (adj. or m. noun)
ⲕⲛ̅ⲧⲉ	Fig (m)	ⲥⲏⲩ	Season (m)
ⲕⲟⲥⲙⲟⲥ	World (m)	ⲱⲛϩ̅	Life (m)
ⲙⲉ	True (adj) or Truth (f)	ϣⲁ	Feast (m)
ⲙⲛ̅ⲧⲣⲉ	(also written ⲙⲛ̅ⲧⲙⲛ̅ⲧⲣⲉ f)	ϣⲉⲗⲉⲉⲧ	Bride (f)
	Testimony	ϣⲱⲥ	Shepherd (m)
ⲙ̅ⲙⲁⲩ	There	ϣⲧⲉⲕⲟ	Prison (m), pl. ϣⲧⲉⲕⲱⲟⲩ
ⲙⲁⲉⲓⲛ	Sign, wonder (m)	ϣⲁϫⲉ	Speech, word (also
ⲙⲁⲁⲩ	Mother (f)		verb 'speak')
ⲟⲉⲓⲕ	Bread (m)	ϩⲓⲏ	Way, road (f)
ⲡ̅ⲛ̅ⲁ̅	Spirit (m), for ⲡⲛⲉⲩⲙⲁ	ϩⲗ̅ⲗⲟ	Old man (f ϩⲗ̅ⲗⲱ)
ⲡⲣⲱ	Winter (f)	ϩⲣⲉ	Food (normally f)
ⲣⲱⲙⲉ	Man	ϩⲟⲟⲩ	Day (m) (C. 730a)

A English into Coptic

1	I am the bread of life	11	He is the Son of man
2	I am the voice	12	It was the feast of the Jews
3	It is the Sabbath	13	They are robbers
4	This is the testimony	14	He was there
5	All mine are thine	15	I am not the Christ
6	We are the seed of Abraham	16	I am in the world
7	I was not there	17	Thou art not the king's friend
8	Thy word is the truth	18	My blood is a true drink
9	My Father is God	19	My Father is in me
10	You are my friends	20	This is the chosen Son of God

B <u>Coptic into English</u>

1 ⲚⲦⲟⳚ ⲡⲉ ⲡⲁⲧⳛⲉⲗⲉⲉⲧ
2 ⲁⲛⲟⲕ ⲡⲉ ⲡⳛⲱⲥ Ⲛⲛⲉⲥⲟⲟⳙ
3 ⲉⲕⳞⳘⲡⲉⳛⲧⲉⲕⲟ
4 ⲟⳙⲡⲚⲁ ⲡⲉ ⲡⲛⲟⳙⲧⲉ
5 ⲚⲧⲱⲧⲚ ⲚⲧⲉⲧⲚ Ⳟⲉⲛⲉⲃⲟⲗ ⳞⳘⲡⲕⲁⳞ
6 ⲛⲉ ⲧⲉⲡⲣⲱ ⲡⲉ
7 ⲡⲉⲭⲥ ⲡⲉ
8 ⲡⲁⲓ ⲡⲉ ⲡⲙⲉⳞⲥⲛⲁⳙ Ⳙⲙⲁⲉⲓⲛ
9 ⲥⲉⳞⳘⲡⲕⲟⲥⲙⲟⲥ
10 ⲧⲁⲥⲃⲱ Ⲛⲧⲱⲓ ⲁⲛ ⲧⲉ
11 ⲁⲛⲄ ⲡⳛⲏⲣⲉ Ⳙⲡⲛⲟⳙⲧⲉ
12 ⲛⲉⲣⲉ ⲧⲙⲁⲁⳙ Ⲛ ⲓ̄ⲥ̄ Ⳙⲙⲁⳙ
13 ⲧⲥⲁⲣⳄ ⲟⳙⳞⲣⲉ Ⳙⲙⲉ ⲧⲉ
14 ϯ ⳞⳘⲡⲁⲉⲓⲱⲧ
15 ⲁⲛⲟⲕ ⲡⲉ ⲧⲉⳞⲓⲏ
16 ⲛⲉ ⲡⲥⲁⲃⲃⲁⲧⲟⲛ ⲡⲉ ⲡⲉⳞⲟⲟⳙ ⲉⲧⳘⲙⲁⳙ
17 Ⲛⲧⲱⲓ ⲁⲛ ⲧⲉ, ⲧⲁⲡⳞⲗⲗⲟ ⲧⲉ
18 ⲁⲅⲁⲑⲟⲛ ⲛⲓⲙ ⲛⲟⳙⳙ ⲡⲉ
19 ⲛⲉ ⲡⲥⲏⳙ ⲁⲛ ⲡⲉ ⲚⲕⲚⲧⲉ
20 ⲟⳙⲁ ⲉⲃⲟⲗ ⲚⳞⲏⲧⲧⲏⳙⲧⲚ ⲟⳙⲇⲓⲁⲃⲟⲗⲟⲥ ⲡⲉ

IX <u>THE VERB</u> (T. § 253ff)

49 There are two basic forms of the verb in Coptic:

A The Infinitive

B The Qualitative

50 A <u>The Infinitive</u>

The infinitive is used to express an <u>event</u> or <u>action</u>. It can possess three forms, although not every verb has all three. The verb ⲕⲱ, (basic meanings 'to place, put, set down, allow' – Crum 94b), has been used to illustrate the forms:

a) the <u>Absolute</u>; ⲕⲱ ; this form is <u>always</u> used before an <u>indirect nominal or pronominal object</u> (§ 93), e.g. ⲁⳙⲕⲱ Ⳙⲙⲟⳙ 'he put him' (Mt. 14.3).

b) the <u>Construct</u>; ⲕⲁ- ; in dictionaries and elsewhere the construct form of a verb, where it exists, is always indicated by a single stroke after the word. The construct form is <u>always</u> used before a <u>direct nominal object</u> (§ 93), e.g. ⲁⳙⲕⲁ ⲡⲙⲏⲏⳛⲉ Ⲛⲥⲱⳙ 'he left the multitude' (Ste. 8.4).

c) the <u>Pronominal</u>; ⲕⲁⲁ= ; indicated by two strokes after the word. This form is used before a <u>direct pronominal object</u>, e.g. ⲁⳙⲕⲁⲁⳙ

23

'he left him' (Till 261.1). The construct and pronominal forms can only be used on a limited number of occasions, see §§ 92-93.

51 B   The Qualitative

ⲔⲎ⁺ ; indicated by the symbol ⁺ after the word. It describes a state or condition. Its usage is limited to the following tenses only: 1st and 2nd Present, Imperfect and Circumstantial, e.g. ⲤⲈⲔⲎ ⳅⲙ̄ⲡⲀⲎⲓ 'they are lying in my house' (Till 266.22).

Not all verbs have a qualitative form. Note ⲚⲎⲨ, qualitative of the verb Ⲉⲓ 'to come', which often has future meaning, even when used with prefixes of the Present tenses, e.g. ⲦⲚ̄ⲚⲎⲨ ⲅⲁⲣ ⲈⳅⲣⲀⲓ ⲈⲚⳓⲓⳍ ⲙ̄ⲡⲚⲞⲨⲦⲈ ⲦⲎⲣⲚ̄   'for we shall all come into the hands of God' (Besa 113.11).

In dictionaries the forms of verbs are given in the order illustrated above; thus Ⲕⲱ appears as Ⲕⲱ , ⲔⲀ- , ⲔⲀⲀ= , ⲔⲎ⁺ .

52 Verbal Classes

The more comprehensive grammars each have a section dealing with the division of verbs into their classes, i.e. 2 lits, 3 lits, etc. Much of this information can be acquired from growing familiarity with the language. Consult, if it is wished, Till, op. cit., § 266ff. and Plumley, op. cit., § 146ff.

53 The Suffix Conjugation (T. § 281ff)

Most verbs in Coptic are conjugated by placing the subject, nominal or pronominal, before the verbal stem (§57). A few verbs, some in very common usage, employ a different method, by which the nominal or pro-nominal subject follows the verbal stem. When the subject is a pronoun the suffix pronouns are used (§5). In the following list of the common-est of these verbs the form for nominal subjects is given first followed by the form used with a pronominal subject.

a) ⲠⲈⳈⲈ-, ⲠⲈⳈⲀ=   'said'; only used with past meaning, e.g. ⲠⲈⳈⲈ ⲚⲈⲨⲙⲀⲑⲎⲦⲎⲤ 'his disciples said' (Mk. 5.31); ⲠⲈⳈⲀⲨ 'they said' (Besa 6.33).

b) ⲛⲉⲥⲉ, ⲛⲉⲥⲱ= 'be beautiful', e.g. ⲛⲉⲥⲱⲥ 'it is beautiful'.

c) ⲛⲁⲛⲟⲩ-, ⲛⲁⲛⲟⲩ= 'be good', exx. ⲛⲁⲛⲟⲩⲥ ⲁⲛ 'it is not good' (Besa 6.33); ⲛⲁⲛⲟⲩ ⲡⲥⲟⲃⲧ̄ 'the wall is good' (Sh. 73.24.21).

d) ⲛⲁⲁ-, ⲛⲁⲁ= 'be great'; apart from this basic meaning it is additionally employed in the compound ⲛⲁⲓⲁⲧ= 'be blessed', when it takes a suffix in agreement with the subject, exx. ⲛⲁⲓⲁⲧⲟⲩ ⲛ̄ⲛ̄ϩⲙ̄ϩⲁⲗ ⲉⲧⲙ̄ⲙⲁⲩ 'blessed are those servants' (Besa 13.31); ⲛⲁⲓⲁⲧϥ̄ 'blessed is he'.

e) ⲛⲁϣⲉ-, ⲛⲁϣⲱ= 'be numerous', exx. ⲛⲁϣⲉ ⲛⲉⲛⲛⲟⲃⲉ 'our sins are many' (Sh. 42.148.22); ⲛⲁϣⲉ ⲛⲉⲧⲙⲟⲩ 'those who die are many' (Sh. 42.74.19).

Note also ϩⲛⲉ-, ϩⲛⲁ= 'be willing'.

Note that no negative construction is possible with ⲡⲉϫⲉ . In order to express 'he did not say' the negative 1st Perfect would be employed (§59).

There are two other verbs which require special mention.

54 a) ⲟⲩⲛ- 'there is' and its negative (ⲙ̄)ⲙⲛ̄- 'there is not'. These are usually employed with an undefined nominal subject (see §§ 45, 58 and 62). To obtain the past tense ⲛⲉ is prefixed, exx. ⲛⲉⲩⲛ ⲟⲩϩⲗ̄ⲗⲟ 'there was an old man' (St. A. 5.11); ⲙ̄ⲙⲛ̄ ⲗⲁⲁⲩ ⲛ̄ⲛⲟⲩϥⲣⲉ 'there is no advantage' (Besa 2.28); ⲟⲩⲛ ϩⲁϩ ⲛⲁϫⲓ ⲥⲃⲱ 'many shall learn' (Besa 2.1); ⲟⲩⲛ ⲟⲩⲕⲗⲏⲣⲟⲛⲟⲙⲓⲁ ϣⲟⲟⲡ 'there is an inheritance' (Besa 8.26); ⲙⲛ̄ ⲗⲁⲁⲩ ⲅⲁⲣ ⲛ̄ⲣⲱⲙⲉ 'for there is no man' (Besa 10.22).

55 b) ⲟⲩⲛⲧⲉ- , ⲟⲩⲛⲧⲁ= 'to have' and its negative ⲙⲛ̄ⲧⲉ- , ⲙⲛ̄ⲧⲁ= 'not to have'.
The object can be direct, exx. ⲟⲩⲛⲧⲁⲩ ⲟⲩⲥⲩⲛⲭⲱⲣⲉⲥⲓⲥ 'they have an excuse' (Sh. 42.28.14); ⲟⲩⲛⲧⲁⲛ ⲟⲩⲛⲟⲙⲟⲥ 'we have a law' (Sh. 73.7.8); ⲙⲛ̄ⲧⲁⲓ ϩⲱⲃ 'I have nothing' (Cha. 27.8), lit. 'I do not have (a) thing'.

Frequently, however, the word ⲘⲘⲀⲨ , 'there', which is untran-
slatable in this context, is inserted between the <u>pronominal</u>
subject and the object. The object is then introduced by Ⲛ̄ ,
exx. ⲞⲨⲚⲦⲀⲨ ⲘⲘⲀⲨ ⲘⲡⲰⲚⲌ̄ 'he has the life' (Jo. 5.24); ⲞⲨⲚⲦⲀⲨ
ⲘⲘⲀⲨ Ⲛ̄ⲞⲨⳠⳘⳘⲉ 'he has a wife' (Budge, Misc. 365.11); ⲞⲨⲚⲦⲀⲨ
ⲘⲘⲀⲨ Ⲛ̄ⲞⲨⲐⲗⲓ⳽ⲓⲥ 'they have an affliction' (Cha. 5.30).

The past tense is formed by prefixing ⲚⲈ , exx. ⲚⲈⲞⲨⲚⲦⲀⲨ ⲘⲘⲀⲨ
Ⲛ̄ⲦⲈⲓⲬⲀⲣⲓⲥ ⳌⲒⲦⲘ̄ⲡⲚⲞⲨⲦⲈ 'he had this favour from God' (Cha. 47.21);
ⲚⲈⲞⲨⲚⲦⲀⲓ ⳌⲰⲰ⳿ Ⲛ̄ⲞⲨⳘⲀⲀⲨ 'I also had a mother' (Cha. 54.31).

If the <u>object</u> is pronominal it is attached to the verbal stem,
even though this means having the suffix subject and object next
to one another, e.g. ⲘⲚ̄ⲦⲀⳘⳙ 'they do not have it' (Sh. 42.90.18).

56   There also exists an abbreviated writing of the pronominal form,
thus; 1 sing. ⲞⲨⲚϯ- , neg. ⲘⲚ̄ϯ- ; 2 sing. m. ⲞⲨⲚⲦⲔ̄- , ⲘⲚ̄ⲦⲔ̄-   ;
2nd sing. f. ⲞⲨⲚⲦⲈ- , ⲘⲚ̄ⲦⲈ- , 3 sing. m. ⲞⲨⲚⲦⲨ̄- , ⲘⲚ̄ⲦⲨ̄-   ;
3 sing. f. ⲞⲨⲚⲦⲤ̄- , ⲘⲚ̄ⲦⲤ̄- ; 1 pl. ⲞⲨⲚⲦⲚ̄- , ⲘⲚ̄ⲦⲚ̄- ; 2 pl.
ⲞⲨⲚⲦⲈⲦⲚ̄- , ⲘⲚ̄ⲦⲈⲦⲚ̄- ; 3 pl. ⲞⲨⲚⲦⲞⲨ- , ⲘⲚ̄ⲦⲞⲨ- .

When this form is used the object is a noun and direct, exx. ⲞⲨⲚϯ-
ⲦⲈⲌ̄ⲞⲨⲤⲓⲀ   'I have the authority' (Jo. 10.18); ⲞⲨⲚⲦⲨ̄ Ⲓ̄Ⲥ̄
'he has Jesus' (Sh. 42.79.11).

Vocabulary

ⲃⲉⲕⲉ	Reward, wage (m)	ⲛⲁ	Pity, charity, mercy (m)
ⲃⲁⲗ	Eye (m)	ⲛ̄ⲕⲁ	Property (m)
ⲇⲁⲓⲙⲟⲛⲓⲟⲛ	Demon (m)	ⲛⲟⲙⲟⲥ	Law (m)
ⲉⲝⲟⲩⲥⲓⲁ	Authority (f)	ⲟⲩⲟⲉⲓⲛ	Light (m)
ⲏⲣⲡ	Wine (m)	ⲟⲩⲱⲧ	Single, alone
ⲕⲁⲥ	Bone (m)	ⲱⲛⲏ	Garden (f)
ⲗⲁⲁⲩ	(+ ⲛ̄-) Anyone, anything; with neg, No-one, nothing	ⲍⲁⲓ	Husband (m)
		ⲍⲓ	Here to be used with the meaning 'or'
ⲙⲁ	Place (m) ⲙⲁⲛ̄ϣⲱⲡⲉ Abode;		
ⲡⲉⲓⲙⲁ	This place, here	ⲍⲙⲟⲩ	Salt (m)
ⲙⲛ̄, ⲛⲙ̄ⲙⲁ=	With (§87)	ⲍⲙ̄ⲍⲁⲗ	Servant (m)
ⲙⲉⲣⲟⲥ	Part (m)	ϫⲟⲓ	Boat, ship (m)
ⲙⲁⲑⲏⲧⲏⲥ	Disciple (m)	ϫⲓ ⲛ̄ϭⲟⲛⲥ̄	Violence (m)
ⲙⲟⲟⲩ	Water (m)	ϭⲉ	Therefore
ⲙⲁⲍ	Nest (m)		

A English into Coptic

1 There is a demon with you

2 There are many abodes

3 There was a man there

4 There was much water in that place

5 There is no-one

6 There is no violence

7 The Son of Man has authority

8 We have no king

9 He had much property

10 Thou hast no part with me

11 They have their nests

12 The salt is good

13 Blessed are your eyes

14 I have five brothers

15 Those said

16 They had no child

17 Your reward is great in heaven

18 Mercy has no bone or flesh

19 He said:[1] 'it is I'

20 I have the testimony

1 To introduce direct speech use ϫⲉ (see §97); this use of ϫⲉ also occurs in section B, no. 18.

B <u>Coptic into English</u>

1	ⲟⲩⲛ ⲟⲩϣⲏⲣⲉ ϣⲏⲙ ⲙ̄ⲡⲉⲓⲙⲁ	11	ⲛⲉ ⲟⲩⲛⲧⲁⲛ ϩⲁϩ
2	ⲙ̄ⲙⲛ̄ ⲇⲁⲓⲙⲟⲛⲓⲟⲛ ⲛ̄ⲙ̄ⲙⲁⲓ	12	ⲟⲩⲛⲧⲉⲧⲛ̄ ⲡⲟⲩⲟⲉⲓⲛ
3	ⲟⲩⲛⲧⲁϥ ⲙ̄ⲙⲁⲩ ⲙ̄ⲡⲱⲛ̄ϩ	13	ⲛⲉⲩⲛ ⲟⲩϣⲛⲏ
4	ⲛⲉⲩⲛ ⲙⲁ	14	ⲛⲉⲩⲛ ⲟⲩⲁ ⲉⲃⲟⲗ ϩⲛ̄ⲛⲉϥⲙⲁⲑⲏⲧⲏⲥ
5	ⲙⲛ̄ⲧⲟⲩ ⲏⲣⲡ	15	ⲟⲩⲛ ϩⲉⲛ ⲛⲟϭ ⲛ̄ⲁⲅⲁⲑⲟⲛ
6	ⲙⲛ̄ⲧⲉⲧⲛ̄ ⲙ̄ⲙⲁⲩ ⲙ̄ⲡⲉϥϣⲁϫⲉ	16	ⲡⲉϫⲉ ⲧⲙⲁⲁⲩ ⲛ̄ ⲓ̄ⲥ̄
7	ⲙ̄ⲙⲛ̄ ϭⲉ ϫⲟⲓ	17	ⲛⲁⲓⲁⲧϥ̄ ⲙ̄ⲡϩⲙ̄ϩⲁⲗ ⲉⲧⲙ̄ⲙⲁⲩ
8	ⲙⲛ̄ϯ ϩⲁⲓ	18	ⲡⲉϫⲁϥ ϫⲉ ⲁⲛⲟⲕ ⲟⲩⲛⲧⲁⲓ ⲙ̄ⲙⲁⲩ ⲛ̄ⲟⲩϩⲣⲉ
9	ⲟⲩⲛϯ ϩⲁϩ ⲛ̄ϣⲁϫⲉ	19	ⲛⲁⲛⲟⲩ ⲡⲛⲟⲙⲟⲥ
10	ⲟⲩⲛⲧⲥ̄ ⲧⲉⲝⲟⲩⲥⲓⲁ	20	ⲛⲁϣⲉ ⲛ̄ϣⲏⲣⲉ

2 In section B, no. 1, translate the ⲙ̄ as 'in'; this is normally expressed by means of the preposition ϩⲛ̄- , (ⲛ̄ϩⲏⲧ= before suffixes).

57 <u>The Prefix Conjugation</u> (T. § 301 ff)

Using the 1st Perfect tense as an example, the pattern normally adopted is:

VERBAL PREFIX	SUBJECT	VERB	
ⲁ	ⲡⲣⲱⲙⲉ	ⲃⲱⲕ	'the man went'
ⲁ	ϥ	ⲃⲱⲕ	'he went'

Exceptions to this rule are the 1st Present and the 1st Future tenses, which have no verbal prefix. This means that with the 1st Present the subject is attached directly to the verb, while with the 1st Future the pattern is subject, ⲛⲁ- , verb.

As regards negation, it will be noted that some tenses have their own negative forms. Others are negated either by ⲛ̄ ..... ⲁⲛ (ⲉⲛ ..... ⲁⲛ with the Circumstantial Present) or by ⲧⲙ̄ . The ⲛ̄ is not always written; where it is it precedes all other elements. ⲁⲛ most commonly comes immediately after the verb, though it can be found relegated to a position later in the sentence.

THE TENSES

58 A <u>1st Present</u>

Sing. 1	ϯ-		Pl. 1	ⲧⲛ̄-		
2m	ⲕ̄-					
2f	ⲧⲉ-		2	ⲧⲉⲧⲛ̄-	Negation	ⲛ̄ ..... ⲁⲛ
3m	ϥ̄-					
3f	ⲥ̄-		3	ⲥⲉ-		

Nominal subject: subject – verb

exx. ⲧⲛ̄ⲉⲡⲉⲓⲑⲏⲙⲓ ⲉⲛⲉϩⲃⲏⲩⲉ ⲙ̄ⲡⲛⲟⲩⲧⲉ ⲁⲗⲗⲁ ⲧⲛ̄ⲙⲛ̄ⲧⲁⲥⲑⲉⲛⲏⲥ ⲁⲙⲁϩⲧⲉ ⲙ̄ⲙⲟⲛ 'we set our hearts to the works of God but our weakness hinders us' (Sh. 42.27.2); ⲡⲁⲛⲁϩⲃⲉϥ ⲅⲁⲣ ϩⲟⲗϭ̄ 'for my yoke is sweet' (Besa 40.24); ⲡⲭⲟⲉⲓⲥ ⲅⲁⲣ ⲙⲟⲩⲧⲉ ⲉⲣⲟⲛ ⲁⲩⲱ ϥ̄ⲥⲟⲡⲥ̄ ⲙ̄ⲙⲟⲛ 'for the Lord calls us and treats us (like children)' (Besa 51.20).

Apart from its simple present meaning there are occasions when the 1st Present has what has been called 'perfect continuous' sense (see D.W. Young, 'On Shenute's Use of Present 1', in <u>J.N.E.S.</u>, Vol. 20 (1961), p. 115ff). In English this would be expressed by 'have/had been doing', i.e. continuous past action carried over to the present, exx. ϯⲥⲟⲟⲩⲛ ⲙ̄ⲙⲟ 'I have known thee' (Sh. 42.21.10); ϯⲱϣ 'I have been reading' (Sh. 42.218.17).

The 1st Present is also used in oaths, e.g. ϥ̄ⲟⲛϩ̄ ⲛ̄ϭⲓ ⲡⲭⲟⲉⲓⲥ 'as the Lord liveth' (Ru. 3.13).

An undefined nominal subject must be introduced by ⲟⲩⲛ- or ⲙⲛ̄; e.g. ⲟⲩⲛ ⲟⲩⲛⲟϭ ⲛ̄ⲭⲁⲥⲙⲁ ⲧⲁⲭⲣⲏⲩ 'a great chasm is fixed' (Lk. 16.26).

59 B <u>1st Perfect</u>

					Negation			
Sing. 1	ⲁⲓ-	Pl.1	ⲁⲛ-		Sing. 1	ⲙ̄ⲡ(ⲉ)ⲓ-	Pl. 1	ⲙ̄ⲡ(ⲉ)ⲛ-
2m	ⲁⲕ-				2m	ⲙ̄ⲡ(ⲉ)ⲕ-		
2f	ⲁⲣⲉ-	2	ⲁⲧⲉⲧⲛ̄-		2f	ⲙ̄ⲡⲉ-	2	ⲙ̄ⲡⲉⲧⲛ̄-
3m	ⲁϥ-				3m	ⲙ̄ⲡ(ⲉ)ϥ-		
3f	ⲁⲥ-	3	ⲁⲩ-		3f	ⲙ̄ⲡ(ⲉ)ⲥ-	3	ⲙ̄ⲡⲟⲩ-

Before nom. subject ⲁ–   Before nom. subject ⲙ̄ⲡⲉ-

Past section, normally of limited duration, exx. ⲁϥⲃⲱⲕ ⲉϩⲟⲩⲛ ⲉⲧⲉⲕⲕⲗⲏⲥⲓⲁ 'he went into the church' (St. A. 4.7); ⲁⲛⲟⲩⲱⲙ ⲉⲃⲟⲗ ϩⲙ̄ⲡⲉⲃⲉⲓⲱ 'we ate from the honey' (Sh. 42.149.21); ⲁϥⲙⲟⲩ ϩⲛ̄ϣⲓⲏⲧ 'he died in Shiēt' (Cha. 19.33); ⲁϥⲧⲱⲟⲩⲛ ⲁϥⲉⲓ ⲉⲃⲟⲗ ⲁⲩⲱ ⲁϥⲭⲓⲧϥ̄ ⲉⲩⲙⲁ ⲁϥⲧⲥⲁⲃⲟⲩ 'he arose, he came out, and he took him to a place (and) he showed him' (Cha. 39.13).

60 C Imperfect

Sing. 1	ⲛⲉⲓ-	Pl. 1	ⲛⲉⲛ-
2m	ⲛⲉⲕ-		
2f	ⲛⲉⲣⲉ-	2	ⲛⲉⲧⲉⲧⲛ̄-
3m	ⲛⲉϥ-		
3f	ⲛⲉⲥ-	3	ⲛⲉⲩ-

Negation (ⲛ̄) ....ⲁⲛ
ⲛ̄ usually omitted

Before nom. subject ⲛⲉⲣⲉ-

As opposed to the 1st Perfect this tense expresses past action of a more continuous nature, exx. ⲛⲉϥϩⲙⲟⲟⲥ 'he was sitting down' (Till 284.18); ⲛⲉϥⲛ̄ⲕⲟⲧⲕ̄ ⲡⲉ 'he was sleeping' (Mt. 8.24); ⲛⲉϥϣⲱⲛⲉ 'he was sick' (Cha. 61.2).

ⲡⲉ often follows the verb when this tense is used, but it has no value in the translation.

61 D 1st Habitude (also termed Praesens Consuetudinis)

					Negation		
Sing. 1	ϣⲁⲓ-	Pl. 1	ϣⲁⲛ-	Sing. 1	ⲙⲉⲓ-	Pl. 1	ⲙⲉⲛ-
2m	ϣⲁⲕ-			2m	ⲙⲉⲕ-		
2f	ϣⲁⲣⲉ-	2	ϣⲁⲧⲉⲧⲛ̄-	2f	ⲙⲉⲣⲉ-	2	ⲙⲉⲧⲉⲧⲛ̄-
3m	ϣⲁϥ-			3m	ⲙⲉϥ-		
3f	ϣⲁⲥ-	3	ϣⲁⲩ-	3f	ⲙⲉⲥ-	3	ⲙⲉⲩ-

Before nom. subject ϣⲁⲣⲉ-   Before nom. subject ⲙⲉⲣⲉ-

This tense is used to express customary or habitual action, or even a state of affairs, but there are occasions when it is difficult, even impossible, to render this idea in the translation, and to this extent the nomenclature of 'Habitude' is not satisfactory. By its very nature the tense has no rigid temporal restrictions; it can describe a state of affairs that prevailed

in the past, that exists in the present (most commonly), or
which will be continued into the future, exx. ⲙⲉϥⲉⲓ ϣⲁ
ⲡⲟⲩⲟⲉⲓⲛ 'he does not come unto the light' (Jo. 3.20); ϣⲁϥⲥⲱⲧⲙ̄
ⲉⲛϣⲁϫⲉ ⲙ̄ⲡⲛⲟⲩⲧⲉ 'he hearkens unto the words of God' (Jo. 8.47);
ⲙⲉⲣⲉ ⲡⲛⲟⲩⲧⲉ ⲥⲱⲧⲙ̄ ⲉⲣⲉⲩⲣ̄ⲛⲟⲃⲉ 'God does not hearken unto (a) sinner'
(Jo. 9.31); ϣⲁϥⲙⲟⲟϣⲉ ϩⲁⲧⲉⲩϩⲏ ⲁⲩⲱ ϣⲁⲣⲉ ⲛ̄ⲉⲥⲟⲟⲩ ⲟⲩⲁϩⲟⲩ ⲛ̄ⲥⲱϥ
'he goes before them, and the sheep follow him' (Jo.10.4);
ϣⲁϥⲧⲁⲙⲓⲟ ⲛ̄ⲛ̄ⲃⲓⲣ 'he used to make baskets' (Till 262.19).

See Young, op. cit., p. 118, note 17, and J. Polotsky in
Orientalistsche Literaturzeitung (1959), p. 460.

62 E 1st Future[1]

Sing. 1 ϯⲛⲁ-   Pl. 1 ⲧⲛ̄ⲛⲁ-
      2m ⲕⲛⲁ-
      2f ⲧⲉⲛⲁ-   2 ⲧⲉⲧⲛ̄ⲛⲁ-   Negation (ⲛ̄) ....ⲁⲛ
      3m ϥⲛⲁ-
      3f ⲥ̄ⲛⲁ-   3 ⲥⲉⲛⲁ-

With a nominal subject the pattern is: subject, ⲛⲁ, verb

Simple future meaning, exx. ⲕⲛⲁⲡⲱⲧ ⲛ̄ⲥⲁⲡϫⲁϫⲉ 'thou shalt pursue
the enemy' (Sh. 42.97.22); ⲡϫⲟⲉⲓⲥ ⲛⲁϫⲓⲕⲃⲁ ⲛ̄ⲟⲩⲟⲛ ⲛⲓⲙ 'the Lord
will take vengeance on everyone' (Sh. 42.137.19); ⲧⲉⲛϩⲓⲏ ⲛⲁⲥⲟⲟⲩⲧⲛ̄
ⲡⲉ ⲁⲩⲱ ⲛ̄ⲧⲛ̄ⲛⲁϫⲓϫⲣⲟⲡ ⲁⲛ 'our way shall be straight
and we shall not stumble' (Besa 76.26).

When the subject is undefined it must be introduced by ⲟⲩⲛ- or ⲙⲛ̄-,
ⲟⲩⲛ ⲟⲩϩⲉⲑⲛⲟⲥ ⲅⲁⲣ ⲛⲁⲧⲱⲟⲩⲛ 'for a nation will arise' (Mk. 13.8);
ⲟⲩⲛ ⲟⲩⲁ ⲛⲁϫⲟⲟⲥ 'one shall say' (Sh. 42.137.5).

1 Students should consult the study of Coptic Future Tenses by
J. Wilson (Mouton, 1970), who concludes that the only true
future tense was the 3rd Future

63 F   <u>3rd Future</u>

Negation

Sing.	1 ⲉⲓⲉ-	Pl.	1 ⲉⲛⲉ-	Sing.	1 ⲛ̄ⲛⲁ-, ⲛ̄ⲛⲉⲓ	Pl.	1 ⲛ̄ⲛⲉⲛ-
	2m ⲉⲕⲉ-				2m ⲛ̄ⲛⲉⲕ-		
	2f ⲉⲣⲉ-		2 ⲉⲧⲉⲧⲛ̄ⲉ-		2f ⲛ̄ⲛⲉ-		2 ⲛ̄ⲛⲉⲧⲛ̄-
	3m ⲉⲩⲉ-				3m ⲛ̄ⲛⲉⲩ-		
	3f ⲉⲥⲉ-		3 ⲉⲩⲉ-		3f ⲛ̄ⲛⲉⲥ-		3 ⲛ̄ⲛⲉⲩ-

Before a nom. subject ⲉⲣⲉ-   Before a nom. subject ⲛ̄ⲛⲉ-

Exceptionally, ...ⲁⲛ can be found negating this tense (<u>Wilson</u>, p. 35).

This tense has a much stronger future sense than the 1st Future. It is used in declarations, avowals, wishes, promises, predictions and, negatively, in prohibitions, exx. ⲡⲭⲟⲉⲓⲥ ⲉⲩⲉⲥⲙⲟⲩ ⲉⲣⲱⲧⲛ̄ ⲁⲩⲱ ⲉⲩⲉ2ⲁⲣⲉ2 ⲉⲣⲱⲧⲛ̄   'the Lord will bless you and guard you' (Besa 33.33); ⲉⲕⲉⲧⲁⲉⲓⲉ ⲡⲉⲕⲉⲓⲱⲧ   'thou shalt honour thy father' (Mt. 19.19); ⲛ̄ⲛⲉ ⲡⲁⲡⲛ̄ⲁ ⲟⲩⲱ2 2ⲛ̄ⲛⲓⲣⲱⲙⲉ   'my spirit shall not dwell in these men' (Besa 33.21).

It is also regularly employed after ⲭⲉ or ⲭⲉⲕⲁⲥ , normally to introduce a final clause (§121), see Wilson, <u>op. cit.</u>, p. 32ff; exx. ⲕⲱ ⲉⲃⲟⲗ ⲙ̄ⲡⲁⲗⲁⲟⲥ ⲭⲉⲕⲁⲥ ⲉⲩⲉϣⲙ̄ϣⲉ ⲛⲁⲓ   'let my people go, that they might serve me' (Sh. 42.84.12); ⲭⲉⲕⲁⲥ ⲉⲥⲉⲥⲟⲟⲩⲧⲛ̄ ⲛ̄ⲛⲉⲕ2ⲓⲟⲟⲩⲉ 'so that it may straighten thy paths' (Pro. 3.6); ⲭⲉ ⲛ̄ⲛⲉⲕϯ ⲛ̄ⲟⲩⲧⲱⲗⲙ̄ ⲙ̄ⲡⲉⲕⲑⲃⲃⲓⲟ   'so that thou shalt not defile thy humility' (Sh. 42.101.22); ⲭⲉ ⲛ̄ⲛⲉⲩϭⲛ̄ ⲡⲉⲧⲥⲟⲟⲩⲛ ⲙ̄ⲙⲟⲟⲩ   'so that they shall not find the one who knows them' (Sh. 42.99.21).

64 G   <u>Potential Future</u>   (also termed the <u>4th Future</u>, <u>Finalis</u> and <u>Future Conjunctive</u>)

The designation used here follows that suggested by L. Th. Lefort in 'A propos de syntaxe copte', in <u>Le Museon</u>, Vol. 60 (1947), p. 7ff.

Sing 1 ⲧⲁ-, ⲧⲁⲣⲓ-   Pl. 1 ⲧⲁⲣⲛ̄-

　　2m ⲧⲁⲣⲉⲕ-

　　2f ⲧⲁⲣⲉ-　　　　　2 ⲧⲁⲣⲉⲧⲛ̄-　　Negation: see below

　　3m ⲧⲁⲣⲉϥ-

　　3f ⲧⲁⲣⲉⲥ-　　　　　3 ⲧⲁⲣⲟⲩ-

Before nom. subject ⲧⲁⲣⲉ-

This tense almost invariably follows imperatives or questions. After imperatives it indicates what will happen if the instruction laid down in the imperative is carried out. When used after, or as part of, a question, its function is less well defined, but it seems to postulate a possible course of action in the future; exx. ⲣⲟⲉⲓⲥ .... ⲧⲁⲣⲛ̄ϭⲛ̄ ⲑⲉ 'be vigilant .... and we shall find the means' (Besa 52.15); ϣⲓⲛⲉ ⲛ̄ⲥⲁⲡⲛⲟⲩⲧⲉ ⲧⲁⲣⲉ ⲧⲉⲧⲙ̄ⲯⲩⲭⲏ ⲱⲛϩ̄ 'seek after God and your soul shall live' (Ps. 68.32); ⲛ̄ⲧⲟⲕ ⲡⲉⲧⲛⲏⲩ ⲭⲛ̄ ⲧⲁⲣⲛ̄ϭⲱϣⲧ̄ ϩⲏⲧϥ̄ ⲛ̄ⲕⲉⲟⲩⲁ 'are you he who is to come, or are we to look for another?' (Mt. 11.13); ⲧⲛ̄ⲛⲟⲟⲩ ⲡⲁⲥⲟⲛ ⲛⲙ̄ⲙⲁⲓ ⲧⲁⲣⲉⲛⲃⲱⲕ ϣⲁ ⲡⲉⲓⲧⲟⲡⲟⲥ 'send my brother with me, and we shall go to this holy place' (Cha. 23.3).

The form ⲧⲁ- for the 1st person singular is the same as that employed by the Conjunctive tense (§ 71). The overlapping functions of these tenses are very noticeable; when translating the Potential Future it is very often necessary to insert 'and', as one does with the Conjunctive.

65　Only one example of a negated Potential Future has come to light; ⲧⲁⲣⲛ̄ϯ ⲭⲛ̄ ⲧⲁⲣⲛ̄ⲧⲙ̄ϯ 'shall we give or shall we not give?' (Mk. 12.14). The use of ⲧⲙ̄- as the negative element is another connection with the Conjunctive tense.

66 H The Optative

Negation

Sing.	1	ⲙⲁⲣⲓ-	Pl.	1	ⲙⲁⲣⲛ̄-	Sing.	1	ⲙ̄ⲡⲣ̄ⲧⲣⲁ-	Pl.	1	ⲙ̄ⲡⲣ̄ⲧⲣⲉⲛ-
	2m	(ⲙⲁⲣⲉⲕ-)					2m	(ⲙ̄ⲡⲣ̄ⲧⲣⲉⲕ-)			
	2f	(ⲙⲁⲣⲉ-)		2	(ⲙⲁⲣⲉⲧⲛ̄-)		2f	(ⲙ̄ⲡⲣ̄ⲧⲣⲉ-)		2	(ⲙ̄ⲡⲣ̄ⲧⲣⲉⲧⲛ̄-)
	3m	ⲙⲁⲣⲉϥ-					3m	ⲙ̄ⲡⲣ̄ⲧⲣⲉϥ-			
	3f	ⲙⲁⲣⲉⲥ-		3	ⲙⲁⲣⲟⲩ-		3f	ⲙ̄ⲡⲣ̄ⲧⲣⲉⲥ-		3	ⲙ̄ⲡⲣ̄ⲧⲣⲉⲩ-

Before nom. subject ⲙⲁⲣⲉ-   Before nom. subject ⲙ̄ⲡⲣ̄ⲧⲣⲉ-

The 2nd person forms do not occur in the classical language, see Lefort, op. cit., p. 22ff.

This tense expresses a wish, exx. ⲙⲁⲣⲉϥⲕⲟⲧϥ̄ ⲉⲡϫⲟⲉⲓⲥ 'let him turn unto the Lord' (Sh. 42.78.7); ⲙⲁⲣⲛ̄ⲥⲱⲧⲙ̄ 'let us hearken' (Besa 20.12); ⲙ̄ⲡⲣ̄ⲧⲣⲉⲛⲁⲙⲉⲗⲉⲓ 'let us not be negligent' (Besa 20.26); ⲙⲁⲣⲛ̄ϯⲉⲟⲟⲩ ⲛ̄ⲧⲟϥ ⲙ̄ⲡⲛⲟⲩⲧⲉ 'rather let us glorify God' (Sh. 73.24.9). A form of the 1st person plural, ⲙⲁⲣⲟⲛ , is used with the meaning 'let us go'.

67 I Future Imperfect

Sing.	1	ⲛⲉⲓⲛⲁ-	Pl.	1	ⲛⲉⲛⲛⲁ-	
	2m	ⲛⲉⲕⲛⲁ-				
	2f	ⲛⲉⲣⲉⲛⲁ-		2	ⲛⲉⲧⲉⲧⲛ̄ⲛⲁ-	Negation ..... ⲁⲛ
	3m	ⲛⲉϥⲛⲁ-				
	3f	ⲛⲉⲥⲛⲁ-		3	ⲛⲉⲩⲛⲁ-	

Before a nom. subject the pattern is ⲛⲉⲣⲉ , subject ⲛⲁ , verb.

This tense is used to describe an event in the past which, at the time, had not taken place, but which is now thought of as completed; in English this would be expressed by 'he was about to .....'. When used in the apodosis of a conditional sentence (§112) it has the meaning 'he would have ....'; exx. ⲛⲉϥⲛⲁⲙⲟⲩ ⲅⲁⲣ ⲡⲉ 'for he was about to die' (Jo. 4.47); ⲛⲉⲛⲛⲁϭⲱ ⲁⲛ ⲡⲉ ϩⲙ̄ⲡⲉⲓⲙⲁ 'we would not have remained here' (Sh. 42.118.15); ⲛⲉⲣⲉ-ⲧⲉⲓⲙⲓⲛⲉ ⲛ̄ⲣⲱⲙⲉ ⲛⲁⲱⲙⲥ̄ 'this kind of man would have been submerged' (Sh. 73.42.3).

As with the Imperfect tense (§ 60), ⲧⲉ is often found after the verb.

EXERCISE III

In this exercise the student encounters for the first time the question of direct or indirect object, and it is suggested that he reads §§ 93–95 before commencing the exercise.

Vocabulary

ⲁϩⲉⲣⲁⲧ= Stand (+ suffix in agreement with the subject – Crum 536b)

ⲃⲱⲕ, ⲃⲁⲕ=, ⲃⲏⲕᵗ Go; + ⲉϩⲟⲩⲛ (ⲉ-) Enter; + ⲉϩⲣⲁⲓ Go up; + ⲉⲃⲟⲗ ϩⲛ̄- Leave (C. 29a)

ⲉⲓ, ⲛⲏⲩᵗ Come; + ⲉⲃⲟⲗ ϩⲛ̄- out from; + ⲉ- come to; + ⲉϩⲟⲩⲛ ⲉ- Come in
   (C. 70a)

ⲉⲓⲃⲉ, ⲟⲃⲉᵗ Thirst

ⲉⲓⲣⲉ, ⲣ̄-, ⲁⲁ=, ⲟᵗ Do, make, act (C. 83a ff)

ⲕⲣⲓⲛⲉ To judge, condemn

ⲙⲉ, ⲙⲉⲣⲉ-, ⲙⲉⲣⲓⲧ= To love (also m. noun)

ⲙⲟⲩ, ⲙⲟⲟⲩⲧᵗ Die

ⲙⲟⲩⲧⲉ Call, summon

ⲙⲟⲩϩ Burn, glow

ⲛⲁⲩ To see

ⲡⲓⲥⲧⲉⲩⲉ Believe

ⲣ̄-ⲙⲛ̄ⲧⲣⲉ Bear witness

ⲣ̄-ⲟⲩⲟⲉⲓⲛ Shine, enlighten

ⲣ-ϭⲱⲃ To be weak

ⲥⲙⲟⲩ, ⲥⲙⲁⲙⲁⲁⲧᵗ Bless, praise, + ⲉ- (ⲉⲣⲟ=) Bless someone

ⲥⲱⲧⲙ̄, ⲥⲉⲧⲙ̄-, ⲥⲟⲧⲙ= Hear; + ⲉ (ⲉⲣⲟ=) Listen to; + ⲛ̄ⲥⲁ- (ⲛ̄ⲥⲱ=) Obey
   (C. 363b)

ⲥⲟⲟⲩⲛ, ⲥⲟⲩⲛ-, ⲥⲟⲩⲱⲛ= Know

ⲧⲁⲙⲓⲟ, ⲧⲁⲙⲓⲉ-, ⲧⲁⲙⲓⲟ=, ⲧⲁⲙⲓⲏⲩᵗ Make, create

ⲧⲁⲙⲟ, ⲧⲁⲙⲉ-, ⲧⲁⲙⲟ= Tell, inform

ⲧⲱⲟⲩⲛ, ⲧⲟⲩⲛ-, ⲧⲱⲟⲩⲛ= Arise

ⲧⲱϩ, ⲧⲉϩ-, ⲧⲁϩ=, ⲧⲏϩᵗ Mix, be mixed

ⲟⲩⲱⲛ, ⲟⲩⲏⲛᵗ Open

ⲥⲧⲁⲩⲣⲟⲩ Crucify (also written ⲥ⳨ⲟⲩ)

35

ⲱⲃϣ̅, ⲟⲃϣ̅ =, ⲟⲃϣ⁺   Forget

ⲱⲗ, ⲟⲗ-, ⲟⲗ =, ⲏⲩ⁺   Hold, contain; + ⲉϩⲟⲩⲛ   Gather in

ⲱⲛϩ̅, ⲟⲛϩ̅⁺   To live

ϣⲓⲛⲉ, ϣⲉⲛ-, ϣⲛ̅ⲧ =   Seek, ask; + ⲛ̅ⲥⲁ- (ⲛ̅ⲥⲱ =) Seek after, inquire
     for; + ⲉ- (ⲉⲣⲟ =) Visit (C. 569a)

ϣⲱⲛⲉ Be sick

ϣⲱⲡⲉ, ϣⲟⲟⲡ⁺   Become, befall; <u>Qual.</u> Be, exist (C. 577b)

ϣⲧⲟⲣⲧⲣ̅, ϣⲧⲣ̅ⲧⲣ̅-, ϣⲧⲣ̅ⲧⲱⲣ =, ϣⲧⲣ̅ⲧⲱⲣ⁺   Be disturbed, troubled

ϣⲟⲩϣⲟⲩ   Boast (verb or m. noun)

ϣⲁϫⲉ Speak; + ⲙⲛ̅- Speak with

ϩⲉ, ϩⲉ-, ϩⲏⲩ⁺   Fall; ϩⲉ ⲉⲃⲟⲗ   Perish; + ⲉ- (ⲉⲣⲟ =) Find (C. 637a)

ϩⲁⲣⲉϩ Guard, keep, be careful

ϩⲟⲧⲉ Fear (f); ⲣ̅-ϩⲟⲧⲉ   To fear; ⲁⲧϩⲟⲧⲉ   Fearless; ϯ-ϩⲟⲧⲉ Terrify

ϫⲱϩⲙ̅, ϫⲉϩⲙ̅-, ϫⲁϩⲙ̅ =, ϫⲁϩⲙ̅⁺   Defile, Pollute

ϭⲱ, ϭⲉⲉⲧ⁺   Remain, continue (803a)

ⲁⲩⲱ	And	ⲡⲟⲗⲓⲥ	City (f)
ⲃⲓⲣ	Basket (m)	ⲣⲁⲛ	Name (m)
ⲓⲱϩⲁⲛⲛⲏⲥ	John	ⲥⲁⲙⲁⲣⲓⲁ	Samaria
ⲕⲁⲣⲡⲟⲥ	Fruit (m)	ⲥⲁⲙⲁⲣⲓⲧⲏⲥ	Samaritan
ⲕⲁⲧⲁ	According to	ⲥⲱⲙⲁ	Body (m)
ⲙⲁⲣⲓⲁ	Mary	ⲥⲱϣⲉ	Field (f)
ⲙⲁⲣⲑⲁ	Martha	ⲥⲁϩ	Teacher (m or f)
(ⲉ)ⲛⲧⲟⲗⲏ	Commandment (f)	ϣⲁ-, ϣⲁⲣⲟ =	Unto (§ 87)
ⲟⲣⲅⲏ	Anger (f)	ϩⲏⲧ	Heart (C.714a)
			ϩⲧⲏ = with suffixes

A   <u>English into Coptic</u>

1 She went into the city

2 For Jew does not mix with Samaritan

3 He did not tell his father

4 He was speaking with a woman

5 Thy son liveth

6 You will seek me

7 John was standing

8 He remained, he did not go

9 They hearken unto my voice

10 Seek (and) ye shall find

11 Let us open our eyes

12 So that I might not thirst

13 Let not your heart be troubled

14 My brother would not have died

15 He shall not perish

16 Let us go unto him

17 You would have done the works of Abraham

18 Arise (and) Christ will enlighten you

B   <u>Coptic into English</u>

1 ⲛⲟⲩⲓ ⲥⲟⲟⲩⲛ ⲙ̄ⲙⲟⲓ

2 ⲟⲩⲛ ⲅⲁϩ ϣⲟⲩϣⲟⲩ

3 ⲁⲩⲉⲓ ⲉⲩⲡⲟⲗⲓⲥ ⲛ̄ⲧⲉⲧⲥⲁⲙⲁⲣⲓⲁ

4 ϣⲁⲩⲙⲟⲩⲧⲉ ⲉⲛⲉⲩⲉⲥⲟⲟⲩ ⲕⲁⲧⲁ ⲛⲉⲩⲣⲁⲛ

5 ⲛⲉⲣⲉ ⲥⲟⲟⲩⲛ ⲁⲛ ⲡⲉ ⲛ̄ⲧⲉⲛⲧⲟⲗⲏ

6 ⲁⲡⲥⲁϩ ⲉⲓ ⲁⲩⲱ ϥ̄ⲙⲟⲩⲧⲉ ⲉⲣⲟ

7 ⲡⲉⲓⲱⲧ ⲛⲁⲕⲣⲓⲛⲉ ⲁⲛ ⲛ̄ⲗⲁⲁⲩ

8 ⲁⲧⲉⲧⲛ̄ ⲛⲁⲩ ⲉⲣⲟⲓ ⲁⲩⲱ ⲛ̄ⲧⲉⲧⲛ̄ ⲡⲓⲥⲧⲉⲩⲉ ⲁⲛ

9 ⲛⲉⲣⲉ ⲓ̅ⲥ̅ ⲙⲉ ⲙ̄ⲙⲁⲣⲑⲁ ⲙⲛ̄ ⲙⲁⲣⲓⲁ

10 ⲧⲁⲥⲧⲁⲩⲣⲟⲩ ⲙ̄ⲡⲉⲧⲛ̄ⲣ̄ⲣⲟ

11 ⲭⲉⲕⲁⲥ ⲉⲩⲉⲣ̄ⲙⲛ̄ⲧⲣⲉ

12 ⲙⲁⲣⲟⲛ ⲉⲃⲟⲗ ϩⲙ̄ⲡⲉⲓⲙⲁ

13 ⲛⲉⲩⲛⲁⲣ̄ ⲛⲉⲩϩⲃⲏⲩⲉ

14 ⲉⲣⲉ ⲡⲭⲟⲉⲓⲥ ⲥⲱⲧⲙ̄ ⲉⲣⲟⲕ

15 ⲙ̄ⲡⲣ̄ⲧⲣⲉϥ ⲣ̄ϭⲱⲃ

16 ⲛⲉⲛⲛⲁⲭⲱϩⲙ̄ ⲁⲛ ⲡⲉ ⲙ̄ⲡⲉⲛⲥⲱⲙⲁ

17 ⲧⲟⲣⲅⲏ ⲙ̄ⲡⲭⲟⲉⲓⲥ ⲛⲁⲙⲟⲩϩ

18 ⲛⲉⲣⲉ ⲟⲩⲣⲱⲙⲉ ϣⲟⲟⲡ ⲙ̄ⲙⲁⲩ ⲛⲉϥϣⲱⲛⲉ

19 ϣⲁⲩⲱⲗ ⲉϩⲟⲩⲛ ⲛ̄ⲛ̄ⲕⲁⲣⲡⲟⲥ ⲛ̄ⲧⲉϥⲥⲱϣⲉ

20 ⲉⲩⲉⲥⲙⲟⲩ ⲉⲣⲟⲟⲩ

68 J   <u>Tenses of Incomplete Action</u>

a)   <u>'Until'</u> (T. § 312)

Sing. 1 ϣⲁⲛϯ-, ϣⲁⲛⲧⲁ-   Pl. 1 ϣⲁⲛⲧⲛ̄-

     2m ϣⲁⲛⲧⲕ̄-

     2f ϣⲁⲛⲧⲉ-   2 ϣⲁⲛⲧⲉⲧⲛ̄-   Negation: see below

     3m ϣⲁⲛⲧϥ̄-

     3f ϣⲁⲛⲧⲥ̄-   3 ϣⲁⲛⲧⲟⲩ-

Before nom. subject ϣⲁⲛⲧⲉ-

exx. ϣⲁⲛⲧⲟⲩϫⲓⲧϥ̄ ⲉϩⲟⲩⲛ ⲉⲛⲉⲩⲏⲉⲓ 'until he is received into their
houses' (Sh. 73.24.4); ϣⲁⲛⲧϥ̄ ⲑⲃⲃⲓⲟ ⲉⲃⲟⲗ   'until he is humbled'
(Besa 18.33); ϣⲁⲛⲧⲟⲩⲥⲱϣ ⲙ̄ⲡⲣⲁⲛ ⲛ̄ⲛⲉⲛⲉⲓⲟⲧⲉ 'until they despised
the name of our fathers' (Besa 63.19).

Occasionally it is used to indicate a result, e.g. ϣⲁⲛⲧϥ̄ϯ ⲛⲁⲩ
ⲙ̄ⲡⲃⲁⲡⲧⲓⲥⲙⲁ 'so that he might baptize them' (P. Cod 12.30)

69   Examples of the negation of ϣⲁⲛⲧⲉ- have only been found with
pronominal subjects, and in these ⲧⲙ̄- is placed before the verb,
e.g. ϣⲁⲛⲧⲟⲩⲧⲙ̄ ⲗⲁⲁⲩ 'until there was no—one left' (Josh. 8.22).

70 b)   <u>'Before, not yet'</u> (T. § 320)

Sing. 1 ⲙ̄ⲡⲁϯ-   Pl. 1 ⲙ̄ⲡⲁⲧ(ⲉ)ⲛ̄-

     2m ⲙ̄ⲡⲁⲧ(ⲉ)ⲕ̄-

     2f ⲙ̄ⲡⲁⲧⲉ-   2 ⲙ̄ⲡⲁⲧⲉⲧⲛ̄-

     3m ⲙ̄ⲡⲁⲧ(ⲉ)ϥ̄-

     3f ⲙ̄ⲡⲁⲧ(ⲉ)ⲥ̄-   3 ⲙ̄ⲡⲁⲧⲟⲩ-

Before nom. subject ⲙ̄ⲡⲁⲧⲉ-

exx. ⲙ̄ⲡⲁⲧⲉ ⲟⲩⲁⲗⲉⲕⲧⲱⲣ ⲙⲟⲩⲧⲉ   'before a cock crows' (Mt. 26.75);
ⲙ̄ⲡⲁⲧⲉⲕⲉⲓⲱⲣϩ̄ ⲙ̄ⲡⲙ̄ⲧⲟⲛ   'you have not yet perceived the contentment'
(Cha. 2.25); ⲙ̄ⲡⲁⲧⲉϥⲉⲓ ⲣⲱ ⲉϩⲣⲁⲓ ⲉⲛϭⲓϫ   'before he falls into the
hands' (Sh. 42.26.11).

71   K   <u>Conjunctive</u> (T. § 321)

Sing.	1	N̄Tⲁ-, Tⲁ-,	Pl.	1	N̄TN̄-
	2m	NF̄-			
	2f	N̄Tⲉ-		2	N̄TⲉTN̄-	Negation: see below
	3m	NⲨ̄-			
	3f	NⲤ̄-		3	N̄Ⲥⲉ-

Before nom. subject   N̄Tⲉ-

If the Copts wanted to join together phrases or sentences they
would normally employ the conjunction ⲁⲩⲱ 'and'; thus 'the man
went and saw' would be rendered as ⲁⲡⲣⲱⲙⲉ ⲃⲱⲕ ⲁⲩⲱ ⲁⲩNⲁⲩ

In certain circumstances, however, they would resort to a special
tense – the Conjunctive:

a)   after the imperative (§ 79). This is the commonest use, exx. TⲱⲟⲩN
NF̄ⲅⲓ M̄ⲡⲉⲕⲋⲗⲟⳓ NF̄ⲙⲟⲟⲩⳉⲉ   'arise, and pick up thy bed, and
walk' (Jo. 5.8); ⲁⲙⲏⲓTN̄ NⲉⲤNⲏⲩ N̄TⲉTN̄ⲤⲱTⲙ̄ ⲉⲩ2ⲁⲡ M̄ⲙⲉ   'come,
brethren, and hearken to a true judgement' (Cha. 37.33); Tⲁⲁⲩ
M̄ⲙN̄TNⲁ N̄TⲉTN̄Tⲁⲙⲓⲟ NⲏTN̄ N̄2ⲉNTⲱⲙⲉ   'give them to charity
and make purses for yourselves' (Besa 40.34).

The Potential Future tense can be used in the same way (see p.33),
but only when there is a promise or threat involved in the obeying
of the imperative, and only with future meaning.

b)   after other tenses, especially the 1st Future, 1st Habitude and
Optative, but only in exceptional circumstances after the 1st
Perfect, exx. †Nⲁⲃⲱⲕ Tⲁⳉⲱ ⲙⲁⲩⲁⲁT 'I will go and remain alone'
(Cha. 10.16); ⲙⲁⲣN̄ⲕTⲟN N̄TN̄ⲁ2ⲉ NⲉN2ⲃⲏⲅⲉ   'let us turn and estab-
lish our works' (Besa 89.13); Ⲭⲉ N̄NⲉNⲣ̄2TⲏN 2N̄TⲉN2ⲁⲏ ⲁⲩⲱ N̄TN̄ⲡⲱ2
M̄ⲡⲉN2ⲏT 2M̄ⲡⲙⲁ   'so that we may not repent at our end and break
our heart in the place' (Besa 83.3); ⳉⲁNTⲉ ⲡⲥⲁTⲁNⲁⲥ ⲙⲉ2ⲉⲓⲁTⳏ M̄ⲙⲱTN̄
ⲁⲩⲱ NⲨ̄2ⲱⲙ ⲉⲭⲱTN̄   'until Satan looks gloatingly at you and
tramples upon you' (Besa 86.14).

c) after certain Greek conjunctions, the commonest being ϩⲱⲥⲧⲉ 'so that', ⲙⲏⲡⲟⲧⲉ, ⲙⲏⲡⲱⲥ 'lest', and ⲉⲓⲙⲏⲧ(ⲉ)ⲓ 'unless', exx. ⲙⲏⲡⲱⲥ ⲟⲛ ⲛ̄ⲥⲉⲭⲟⲟⲥ ⲛⲁⲛ 'lest they also say to us' (Besa 28.15); ⲙⲏⲡⲟⲧⲉ ⲛ̄ⲧⲁⲉⲓ ϣⲁⲣⲱⲧⲛ̄ 'lest I come unto you' (Besa 22.2); ϩⲱⲥⲧⲉ ⲛ̄ⲧⲉⲡⲉϩⲣⲟⲟⲩ ⲛ̄ⲧⲉⲧⲛ̄ⲙⲛ̄ⲧϭⲱⲃ ⲙⲉϩⲡ̄ⲧⲙⲉ 'so that the sound of your weakness filled the village' (Sh. 42.21.14); ⲉⲓⲙⲏⲧⲉⲓ ⲛ̄ⲧⲛ̄ϯ ⲟⲩⲃⲏⲛ 'unless we oppose ourselves' (Sh. 42.107.9).

d) the Conjunctive is sometimes used to introduce a final clause, exx. ⲛ̄ⲧⲁⲓⲉⲓ ϣⲁⲣⲟⲕ ⲧⲁⲛⲁⲩ ⲉⲡⲉⲕϩⲟ 'unto thee have I come (that) I might see thy face' (Till 305.15); ⲁⲭⲓⲥ ⲙ̄ⲡⲁⲥⲟⲛ ⲛ̄ϥⲡⲉϣ ⲧⲉⲕⲗⲏⲣⲟⲛⲟⲙⲓⲁ 'speak to my brother (that) he might divide the inheritance' (Lk. 12.13).

72   ## Negation of the Conjunctive

With a pronominal subject the pattern is subject, ⲧⲙ̄, verb; exx. ⲥⲉⲛⲁϩⲉ ⲛ̄ⲥⲉⲧⲙ̄ⲉϣϭⲙ̄ϭⲟⲙ ⲉⲧⲱⲟⲩⲛ 'they shall fall and be unable to arise' (Besa 33.27); ⲛ̄ⲥⲉⲧⲙ̄ⲧⲁⲙⲟⲓ 'and they do not tell me' (Sh. 42.139.18).

With a nominal subject the pattern is not consistent. Normally one finds ⲛ̄ⲧⲉ, ⲧⲙ̄, subject, verb, exx. ϩⲱⲥⲧⲉ ⲛ̄ⲧⲉⲧⲙ̄ ⲡⲕⲁϩ ϣⲟⲡϥ̄ ⲉⲣⲟϥ 'so that the earth did not receive him' (Cha. 55.13); ⲛ̄ⲧⲉⲧⲙ̄ⲉⲡⲉⲓⲑⲩⲙⲓⲁ ϭⲛ̄ⲙⲁ 'and (the) desire found no place' (Sh. 73.166.15). Occasionally, however, the nominal subject intrudes between ⲛ̄ⲧⲉ and ⲧⲙ̄, exx. ϩⲱⲥⲧⲉ ⲛ̄ⲧⲉ ϩⲁϩ ⲛ̄ⲧⲉ ⲛⲉⲧϩⲙ̄ ⲡⲧⲙⲉ ⲧⲙ̄ⲉϣϭⲙ̄ϭⲟⲙ ⲉⲧⲱⲙⲛ̄ⲧ ⲉⲣⲟϥ 'so that many of the villagers were unable to meet him' (Cha. 54.26); ⲛ̄ⲧⲉ ⲡⲕⲱϩⲧ̄ ⲧⲙ̄ⲉⲛⲉⲣⲅⲉⲓ 'and the fire had no power'.

73   Sometimes the conjunction ⲁⲩⲱ is found accompanying the Conjunctive tense, but it merely reinforces and is not expressed in the translation.

74 L   The Second Tenses (T.§302)

The lst Present, Perfect, Habitude and Future tenses each have a secondary form. These are called 'Second Tenses', and their special function has been identified by H.J. Polotsky in his important work Études de syntaxe copte (1944), p. 21ff. They are employed when there is a desire to stress an adverbial expression, which will usually be found at the end of the sentence. This emphasis is sometimes difficult to express in English, but it is most important that, whenever possible, this function of the second tenses be rendered in the translation. Almost inevitably there are occasions when the above rule does not seem to apply, but in general its application is remarkably consistent.

These second tenses take the following forms:

	Present	Perfect	Habitude	Future
Sing. 1	ⲉⲓ-	ⲛ̄ⲧⲁⲓ-	ⲉⲩⲁⲓ-	ⲉⲓⲛⲁ-
2m	ⲉⲕ-	ⲛ̄ⲧⲁⲕ-	ⲉⲩⲁⲕ-	ⲉⲕⲛⲁ-
2f	ⲉⲣⲉ-	ⲛ̄ⲧⲁⲣⲉ-	ⲉⲩⲁⲣⲉ-	ⲉⲣⲉⲛⲁ-
3m	ⲉⲩ-	ⲛ̄ⲧⲁⲩ-	ⲉⲩⲁⲩ-	ⲉⲩⲛⲁ-
3f	ⲉⲥ-	ⲛ̄ⲧⲁⲥ-	ⲉⲩⲁⲥ-	ⲉⲥⲛⲁ-
Pl.1	ⲉⲛ-	ⲛ̄ⲧⲁⲛ-	ⲉⲩⲁⲛ-	ⲉⲛⲛⲁ-
2	ⲉⲧⲉⲧⲛ̄-	ⲛ̄ⲧⲁⲧⲛ̄-	ⲉⲩⲁⲧⲉⲧⲛ̄-	ⲉⲧⲉⲧⲛ̄(ⲛ)ⲁ-
3	ⲉⲩ-	ⲛ̄ⲧⲁⲩ-	ⲉⲩⲁⲩ-	ⲉⲩⲛⲁ-
Nom. Sub.	ⲉⲣⲉ-	ⲛ̄ⲧⲁ-	ⲉⲩⲁⲣⲉ-	ⲉⲣⲉ....ⲛⲁ

Negation: with the 2nd Present ⲛ̄ .....ⲁⲛ , with the others .....ⲁⲛ .

exx. ⲟⲩⲟⲛ ⲅⲁⲣ ⲛⲓⲙ ⲉⲛⲧⲁⲩϫⲓ ⲥⲏⲩⲉ ⲉⲩⲛⲁϩⲉ ⲉⲃⲟⲗ ϩ̄ⲛ̄ⲧⲥⲏⲩⲉ 'for everyone who has taken up the sword, by the sword shall they perish' (Mt. 26.53), not ' .... they will perish by the sword'; ⲉⲩⲁⲩⲙⲉⲣⲓⲧϥ̄ ⲛ̄ⲧⲟⲩ ⲛ̄ϩⲟⲩⲟ 'but even more does he love him' (Sh. 42.40.11), not 'he loves him more'; ⲛ̄ⲧⲁⲩϣⲓⲛⲉ ϩ̄ⲛ̄ⲟⲩⲙⲛ̄ⲧϩⲁⲕ 'prudently did he ask (Sh. 42.33.8), not 'he asked prudently'; ⲈⳠⲚⲀϯϭⲞⲘ ⲚⲎⲦⲚ̅ ⲦⲎⲢⲦⲚ̅   'unto all of you will he give power' (Besa 89.24); Ⲛ̅ⲦⲀⳠⲢ̅ⳡⲘ̅ⲘⲞ ⲈⲢⲰⲦⲚ̅ ⲈⲦⲂⲈ ⲚⲈⲨ2ⲂⲎⳡⲈ ⲈⲐⲞⲞⳞ 'through their evil works they have become strangers unto you' (Sh. 42.143.13); ⲈⳡⲀⲢⲈ Ⲛ̅ⲢⲰⲘⲈ ⳞⲈ Ⲉ2Ⲙ̅ⲠⲔⲀ2 ⲈⲦⲂⲈ ⲐⲞⲦⲈ   'through fear men fall upon the ground' (Sh. 42.39.9).

Second tenses can also be used in questions, see §§ 99, 104 and 107ii).

75 M The Circumstantial Tenses (also called Umstandssatz) (T. § 328ff)

The subordinate, or circumstantial, clause in English, i.e. 'the man sat down, being tired', 'he stood up, having finished eating', etc., is expressed in Coptic by placing Ⲉ- in front of the verbal prefix or the negatival Ⲛ̅ , although in the latter instance it is not always written. The tenses where this construction is not possible are the Future Imperfect, the Optative, the Potential Future, ⳡⲀⲚⲦⲈ- , the Past Temporal (§118) and the Conjunctive (also ⲠⲈⲬⲈ-).

exx. ⲀⳞⲞⳞⲀ2ⲞⳞ Ⲛ̅ⲤⲰ[Ⳡ]ⲈⲀⳞⲔⲰ Ⲛ̅ⲤⲰⲞⳞ Ⲙ̅ⲠⲈⳞⳘⲞⲒ 'they followed him, having left their boat' (Sh. 42.99.14); ⲈⲚⲈⳞⲞ Ⲛ̅Ⲛ̅ⲞⳞⳡⲎ Ⲛ̅ⲢⲞⲈⲒⲤ Ⲛ̅2Ⲁ2 Ⲛ̅ⲤⲞⲠ ⲈⲘⲈⳞⳞⲰⲂⳘ̅ 'often keeping vigils, not sleeping' (St. A. 11.12); 2Ⲁ2 Ⲛ̅ⲤⲞⲠ ⲈⲘⲚ̅2ⲰⲂ 2Ⲛ̅ⲚⲈⲚϬⲒⳞ 'often there being nothing in our hands' (Sh. 42.110.8); ⲞⳞⲂⲀⲖⲈ ⲠⲈ ⲈⲚⳠⲚⲀⳞ ⲈⲂⲞⲖ ⲀⲚ ⲈⲀⳞⳘⲒ Ⲛ̅ⲞⳞⲂⳡⲈ Ⲙ̅ⲠⲦ̅Ⲃ̅ⲂⲞ 'he is a blind man, seeing not, having forgotten the cleansing' (Besa 74.16).

It is also possible for non-verbal clauses to be prefixed by the circumstantial Ⲉ- , exx. ⲈⲀⲚⲄ̅ ⲞⳞⲤ2ⲒⲘⲈ Ⲛ̅ⲤⲀⲘⲀⲢⲒⲦⲎⲤ 'I being a Samaritan woman' (Jo. 4.9); Ⲉ2ⲈⲚⲬⲢⲎⲤⲦⲞⲤ Ⲛ̅ⲢⲰⲘⲈ ⲚⲈ 'they being good men' (Sh. 42.128.20); ⲈⲀⲚⲞⲚ 2ⲈⲚⲀⲤⲈⳂⲎⲤ 'we being godless' (Sh. 42.149.20)

Two Circumstantial tenses require special mention.

76 a) The Circumstantial Present

Sing.	1	ⲈⲒ-	Pl.	1	ⲈⲚ-	
	2m	ⲈⲔ-				
	2f	ⲈⲢⲈ-		2	ⲈⲦⲈⲦⲚ̅-	Negation ⲈⲚ.....ⲀⲚ
	3m	ⲈⳠ-				
	3f	ⲈⲤ-		3	ⲈⳞ	

Before nom. subject ⲈⲢⲈ-

This tense is widely employed in subordinate clauses which have the same setting in time as the main clause, exx. ⲁⲓⲟⲩⲱϣⲃ ⲉⲓⲭⲱ ⲙⲙⲟⲥ 'I answered, saying' (Sh. 42.27.5); ⲁϥⲉⲓ ⲉϥⲣⲓⲙⲉ 'he came, weeping' (Cha. 6.13); ⲁⲩⲛⲁⲩ ⲉⲣⲟϥ ⲉϥⲙⲟⲟⲛⲉ ⲛⲛⲣⲓⲣ 'they saw him feeding the pigs' (Cha. 29.9); ⲁⲥⲱ ⲉⲥϩⲟⲥⲉ 'she remained troubled' (Cha. 23.27).

The circumstantial clause can precede the main clause, exx. ⲉⲩⲟⲩⲱⲙ ⲇⲉ ϩⲓⲟⲩⲥⲟⲡ ⲡⲉⲭⲁϥ 'while they were once eating he said' (Cha. 24.16); ⲉⲩϩⲙⲟⲟⲥ ⲉⲩⲟⲩⲱⲙ ⲛⲟⲩⲟⲉⲓϣ ⲛϭⲓ ⲛϩⲗⲗⲟ ⲛⲉϥⲁϩⲉⲣⲁⲧϥ 'while the old men were once sitting (and) eating he stood up' (Cha. 25.12).

It can be seen that the verbs in the main and circumstantial clauses are often very closely linked, and in some cases they virtually merge, exx. ⲛⲧⲉⲣⲉϥⲟⲩⲱ ⲉϥⲉⲓⲱ 'when he had finished washing'; ⲁϥϣⲱⲡⲉ ⲉϥⲣⲟⲟⲩⲧ 'he was eager' (Cha. 10.6).

The tense is often used to compensate for a shortage of true adjectives, exx. ⲟⲩⲧⲁⲡⲣⲟ ⲉⲥϭⲟⲟⲙⲉ 'a crooked mouth' (Pro. 4.24) lit. 'a mouth, it being crooked'; ⲗⲁⲁⲩ ⲙⲙⲉⲉⲩⲉ ⲉϥⲭⲁϩⲙ 'any impure thought' (Besa 11.22); ⲟⲩⲙⲏⲏϣⲉ ⲉϥⲟϣ 'a large multitude' (Mk. 3.7).

The Circumstantial Present also has a function in relative clauses, see § 123.

The forms of the Circumstantial Present are the same as those of the 2nd Present. Context will normally clearly indicate which is being used.

77 b) <u>The Future Circumstantial</u>

Sing.	1	ⲉⲓⲛⲁ-	Pl.	1	ⲉⲛⲛⲁ-	
	2m	ⲉⲕⲛⲁ-				
	2f	ⲉⲣⲉⲛⲁ-		2	ⲉⲧⲉⲧⲛ(ⲛ)ⲁ-	Negation: not attested
	3m	ⲉϥⲛⲁ-				
	3f	ⲉⲥⲛⲁ-		3	ⲉⲩⲛⲁ-	

Before nom. subject the pattern is ⲉⲣⲉ , subject, ⲛⲁ , verb

43

This tense describes something 'about to happen'. When used with past reference it complements the Future Imperfect tense, being used in circumstantial clauses where the latter could not be employed. Two occurrences of the same clause illustrate this difference; ⲚⲈⲣⲉⲡϨⲘ̄Ϩⲁⲗ ⲙⲟⲕϨ ⲈⲩⲚⲀⲘⲞⲨ 'the slave was sick, being on the point of dying' (Lk. 7.2); ⲚⲈⲩⲚⲀⲘⲞⲨ ⲅⲁⲣ ⲡⲉ 'for he was on the point of dying' (Jo. 4.47). Other exx. Ⲛ̄ⲦⲈⲣⲈⲤⲈⲓ ⲆⲈ ⲈⲤⲚⲀⲘⲓⲤⲈ 'and when she had come, being about to give birth' (Cha. 23.26); ϨⲦⲞⲞⲨⲈ ⲆⲈ ⲈⲩⲚⲀⲔⲞⲦⲩ̄ ⲈϨⲣⲀⲓ ⲈⲦⲡⲟⲗⲓⲤ ⲀⲩϨⲔⲟ 'in the morning, being about to return to the city, he hungered' (Mt. 21.18).

Occasionally a future action is envisaged in the present, e.g. ⲈⲦⲈⲦⲚ̄Ⲁⲱⲗⲏⲗ 'when you are about to pray' (Lk. 11.2).

78 N Tenses with ⲚⲈ (also called the Praeteritum) (T. § 327)

In non-verbal sentences with nominal predicate the placing of ⲚⲈ at the beginning of the sentence rendered the past tense. Set before certain of the verbal prefixes it has the same function; its use is rather limited, the following tenses being excluded: Imperfect, Future Imperfect, 3rd Future, Optative, Potential Future, ⲱⲀⲚⲦⲈ-, Past Temporal, Conjunctive and the 2nd Tenses. When used with the 1st Perfect tense and Ⲙ̄ⲡⲀⲦⲈ- it produces a pluperfect sense; exx. ⲚⲈⲀⲩⲀϨⲈ ⲅⲁⲣ ⲈⲣⲀⲧⲩ̄ ϨⲚ̄ⲦⲈⲔⲔⲗⲏⲤⲓⲀ 'for he had been standing in the church' (Sh. 42.37.4); ⲚⲈⲩⲀⲩⲡⲀⲣⲀⲦⲏⲣⲈⲓ ⲆⲈ ⲈⲦⲘ̄ⲦⲈϨⲤⲚⲈϨ Ⲉⲣⲟⲩ 'he had been careful not to anoint himself' (St. A. 11.22); ⲚⲈⲀⲩⲦⲱⲂⲀϨ ⲅⲁⲣ Ⲙ̄ⲡⲬⲞⲈⲓⲤ 'for he had prayed unto the Lord' (Cha. 7.6).

79 The Imperative (T. § 297 ff)

This is expressed in the following ways:

a) commonly, by the simple infinitive, exx. ⲤⲰⲦⲘ̄ 'hearken', Ⲩⲓ 'take', etc.

b) verbs beginning with the causative Ⲧ (T. § 276) often have the imperative prefix ⲘⲀ (from ϯ 'to give'), exx. ⲘⲀⲦⲀⲘⲞⲚ 'tell us' (Sh. 42.137.9); ⲘⲀⲦⲤⲀⲂⲞⲓ 'teach me'.

c) with a few verbs by prefixing the letter ⲁ-: ⲁⲛⲁⲩ 'see, behold'; ⲁⲝⲱ 'say' (ⲁⲝⲓ- , ⲁⲝⲓ꞊ before direct objects); ⲁⲩⲱⲛ (an abbreviated writing of ⲁⲟⲩⲱⲛ) 'open'.

d) a few important verbs have irregular forms:

Inf.	IMPERATIVE					
	Masc.	Fem.	Plural	Nom Direct	Pronom Direct	Meaning
ⲉⲓ	ⲁⲙⲟⲩ	ⲁⲙⲏ	ⲁⲙⲏⲉⲓⲧⲛ̄			Come!
ⲉⲓⲛⲉ	ⲁⲛ(ⲉ)ⲓⲛⲉ			ⲁⲛⲓ-	ⲁⲛⲓ꞊	Bring!
ⲉⲓⲣⲉ	ⲁⲣⲓⲣⲉ			ⲁⲣⲓ-	ⲁⲣⲓ꞊	Do!
ⲗⲟ	ⲁⲗⲟⲕ	ⲁⲗⲟ	ⲁⲗⲱⲧⲛ̄			Cease!
ϯ	ⲙⲁ				ⲙⲁ꞊	Give!

The imperative is negated by ⲙ̄ⲡⲣ̄-, placed immediately before the verb, exx. ⲙ̄ⲡⲣ̄ϫⲛⲟⲩⲟⲩ 'do not question them'; ⲙ̄ⲡⲣ̄ⲣ̄ⲡⲱⲃϣ̄ 'do not be forgetful' (Cha. 17.6); ⲙ̄ⲡⲣ̄ⲥⲱ 'do not drink' (Cha. 38.28).

Compound verbs incorporating the verb ⲣ̄ have an imperative form ⲁⲣⲓ- , e.g. ⲁⲣⲓⲡⲙⲉⲉⲩⲉ 'remember' (from ⲣ̄-ⲡ̅ⲙⲉⲉⲩⲉ).

EXERCISE IV
Vocabulary

ⲉⲓⲛⲉ, ⲛ̄-, ⲛ̄ⲧ꞊   Bring (C. 78b)

ⲙⲉⲧⲁⲛⲟ(ⲉ)ⲓ Repent; ⲙⲉⲧⲁⲛⲟⲓⲁ Repentence (f)

ⲙⲟⲟϣⲉ Walk, travel

ⲛ̄ⲕⲟⲧⲕ̄ Sleep

ⲛⲟⲩϫⲉ, ⲛⲉϫ-, ⲛⲟϫ꞊, ⲛⲏϫ⁺   Throw, cast; +ⲉⲃⲟⲗ ϩⲛ̄-(ⲛ̄ϩⲏⲧ꞊)   Cast forth
    from (C. 247a)

ⲡⲁⲣⲁⲃⲁ Transgress

ⲣⲁϣⲉ Rejoice; +ⲉ- Rejoice at, over; <u>m. noun</u> Gladness, joy

ⲥⲱ, ⲥⲁ-, ⲥⲟⲟ꞊   Drink

ϯ, ϯ-, ⲧⲁⲁ꞊, ⲧⲟ⁺   Give (C. 392a); +ⲉ- Give to; +ⲉⲃⲟⲗ Give forth;
    +ⲉϩⲣⲁⲓ ⲉ- Commit to

ⲧⲛ̄ⲛⲟⲟⲩ, ⲧⲛ̄(ⲛ)ⲉⲩ-, ⲧⲛ̄(ⲛ)ⲟⲟⲩ꞊   Send

ϯⲥⲟ	Spare, refrain
ⲟⲩⲱϣⲧ̄	Worship, greet
ⲱⲥⲕ̄, ⲟⲥⲕ̄⁺	Delay, be prolonged
ⲱϩⲥ̄	Reap, mow; <u>m. noun</u> Harvest

ϩⲱⲛ, ϩⲟⲛ=, ϩⲏⲛ⁺ + ⲉϩⲟⲩⲛ ⲉ- (ⲉⲣⲟ=)   Approach, draw near

ϫⲱ, ϫⲉ-, ϫⲟⲟ=   Say (C. 754a) (see §95)

ϫⲱⲕ, ϫⲉⲕ-, ϫⲟⲕ=, ϫⲏⲕ⁺   Complete, finish, be completed, full;
     usually + ⲉⲃⲟⲗ   (C. 761a)

ⲁⲅⲅⲉⲗⲟⲥ	Angel (m)	ⲟⲛ	Again, also
ⲇⲓⲕⲁⲓⲟⲥⲩⲛⲏ	Justice (f)	ⲥⲓⲙⲱⲛ	Simon
ⲉⲥⲏⲧ	Ground (m)	ⲥⲏⲩⲉ	Sword, knife (f)
ⲉⲡⲉⲥⲏⲧ	Downwards, down		Also written ⲥⲏⲃⲉ
ⲉⲧⲃⲉ-, ⲉⲧⲃⲏⲏⲧ=	Because of, concerning (§ 87)	ϯⲙⲉ	Village (m)
		ⲧⲱⲣⲉ	Hand (f); with
ⲉϫⲛ̄-, ⲉϫⲱ=	upon (§ 87)		suffixes ⲧⲟⲟⲧ=
ⲏ(ⲉ)ⲓ	House (m)		(C. 425a)
ⲓⲟⲩⲇⲁⲥ	Judas	ⲧⲟⲟⲩ	Mountain (m)
ⲓⲱⲥⲏⲫ	Joseph	ⲑⲁⲗⲁⲥⲥⲁ	Sea (f)
ⲕⲱϩⲧ̄	Fire (m)	ⲟⲩⲟ(ⲉ)ⲓ	Course (m)
ⲛⲟⲃⲉ	Sin (m);	ϯⲟⲩⲟ(ⲉ)ⲓ	Go about
ⲣ̄-ⲛⲟⲃⲉ	To sin	ⲟⲩⲛⲟⲩ	Hour (f)

A English into Coptic

1 Until they repent

2 Unless he sees the Father

3 Unto my Father will I go

4 I saw the spirit coming down

5 Call thy husband and come here

6 Lest we perish

7 I will go and come again

8 Out of thine (own) mouth will
   I condemn you

9 They had given a commandment

10 They saw Jesus walking upon the
   sea, having approached the ship

11 Come and behold a man of God

12 (It is) because of my sins
   that these thing happen

13 Until their year is finished

14 It is I, do not fear

15 Joseph, being a disciple of Jesus

16 I will cast you (f) out and my
   eye will not spare you

17 O Lord, come down before my son
   dies

18 My hour has not yet come

19 Do not transgress the commandment of God

20 Upon this mountain did our fathers worship

B Coptic into English

1 ⲚⲦⲀⲒⲈⲒ ⲀⲚ ⳰ⲚⲦⲠⲈ

2 ⲚⲈⲘⲠⲀⲦ⳰ⲨⲈⲒ ⲈⳢⲞⲨⲚ ⲈⲠⳲ⳦⳩⳩Ⲉ

3 ⳩ⲏⲠⲰⲤ ⲚⲨⲈⲒ ⲚⳡⲈ ⲈⲢⲞⲚ

4 ⲈⲒⲈⲚⲀⲨ ⲈⲦ⳰⳩ⲚⲦⲈⲢⲞ ⳰⳩ⲠⲚⲞⲨⲦⲈ
   ⳰ⲚⲦⲀⲦ⳰⳩ⲂⲰⲔ ⲈⳢⲞⲨⲚ

5 ⲀⲚⲀⲨ, ⳰ⲚⲦⲀⲨⲦ⳰ⲚⲞⲞⲨⲔ ⳩ⲀⲔⲈⲞⲨⲀ ⳰ⲚⲚⲈⲤⲚⲎⲨ

6 ⲚⲈⲀⲨⲂⲰⲔ ⲈⳢⲢⲀⲒ ⲈⲦⲠⲞⲖⲒⲤ

7 ⲀⲨⲈⲒ ⲈⲂⲞⲖ ⲈⲨⲚⲀⲂⲰⲔ ⲈⲠⲰⳢⳲ

8 ⲈⲨⲚⲀ⳩ⲞⲨ Ⳳⲁ-(§ 87) ⲠⲈⲨⲚⲞⲂⲈ

9 ⲀⲢⲒⳤ ⲈⲦⲂⲎⲎⲦ⳰Ⳮ ⲚⲊⲦ⳰⳩Ⲱⳤ⳰Ⳮ

10 ⳰ⲚⲦⲀⲨ⳦Ⲉ ⲠⲀⲒ ⲈⲦⲂⲈ ⲠⲈ⳰ⲠⲚⲀ

11 ⳰⳩ⲠⳲⲢⲤⲰ ⳰⳩ⲠⲈⲒ⳩ⲞⲞⲨ

12 ⲀⲨⲂⲰⲔ ⲈⲠⲈⲨⲎⲒ ⲈⲨⲢⲀ⳩Ⲉ

13 ⳰⳩ⲠⲀⲦⲈⲨ ⲠⲀⲢⲀⲂⲀ ⳰ⲚⲦ⳰ⲚⲦⲞⲖⲎ

14 ⲚⲈⳤⲦⲞⲨⲞⲒ Ⲉⳤ⳩ⲒⲚⲈ ⳰ⲚⳤⲰⲨ

15 ⲈⲢⲈ ⲦⲀ⳦ⲒⲔⲀⲒⲞⲤⲨⲚⲎ ⲚⲎⲨ (§ 51) ⲈⲂⲞⲖ Ⳣ⳰Ⲛ ⲢⲰⳤ

16 ⲀⲚⲒⲚⲈ ⳰ⲚⲦⲈⲒⲮⲨ⳦Ⲏ ⲈⲂⲞⲖ ⳩ⲀⲢⲞⲚ

17 ⲒⲞⲨⲆⲀⳤ Ⲡ⳩ⲎⲢⲈ ⳰ⲚⳤⲒ⳩ⲰⲚ, ⲈⲞⲨⲀ ⲠⲈ
   ⲈⲂⲞⲖ Ⳣ⳰⳩Ⲡ ⳰⳩⳰ⲚⲦⳤⲚⲞⲞⲨⳤ

18 ⲂⲰⲔ ⲚⲊ⳰ⲚⲔⲞⲦ⳰Ⳮ ⳩ⲀⲚⲦⲈⲨⲈⲒ

19 Ⲁ⳩Ⲏ ⳰ⲚⲦⲈⲚⲀⲨ ⲈⲦⲞⲨ ⲔⲈ⳩ⲀⲀⲨ

20 ⲀⲒⲚⲀⲨ ⲈⲨⲀⲅⲅⲈⲖⲞⳤ ⳰ⲚⲦⲈⲠ⳦ⲞⲈⲒⳤ ⲈⳢⲞⲨⲚ
   ⲞⲨⳤⲀ⳩Ⲉ ⳰ⲚⲔⲰⳢⳲ ⳰ⲚⲦⲞⲞⲦ⳰⳨

X THE INFINITIVE (T. § 335ff)

80 The infinitive has two forms:

  a) The Simple Infinitive, i.e. 'to hear', 'to go', etc.

  b) The Causative Infinitive, i.e. 'to cause to hear', etc.

81 The Simple Infinitive can take one of a number of prefixes:

  a) when functioning as a noun it can be preceded by the masculine
      definite article, the indefinite article, the demonstrative pro-
      noun, or possessive adjective, exx. ⲡⲁⲣⲟⲟⲩϣ 'my concern' (Sh.
      42.24.5); ⲡϫⲱϩⲙ ⲡⲉ ⲙⲛ̄ⲡⲥⲱⲱϣ ⲙⲛ̄ⲡϫⲓⲟⲩⲉ ⲙⲛ̄ⲡϭⲟⲗ 'pollution, defilement,
      theft, and lying' (Besa 46.16); ϩⲉⲛⲕⲓⲙ ⲛ̄ⲃⲁⲗ ⲁⲩⲱ ϩⲉⲛϫⲱⲣⲙ̄ ⲛ̄ⲧⲏⲏⲃⲉ
      'winkings of (the) eye and beckonings with (the) finger' (Besa
      47.8); ⲡⲉⲕⲟⲩϫⲁⲓ 'thy salvation' (Lk. 2.30).

  b) the preposition ϩⲛ̄- + the indefinite article ⲟⲩ , giving an
      adverbial expression, exx. ϩⲛ̄ⲟⲩⲣⲁϣⲉ 'joyfully' (Cha. 61.27),
      lit. 'with a rejoicing'; ϩⲛ̄ⲟⲩⲑⲃ̄ⲃⲓⲟ 'humbly' (Cha. 24.19);
      ϩⲛ̄ⲟⲩⲱⲣϫ̄ 'safely' (Mk. 14.44).

      This construction can also be used for emphasis, e.g. ϩⲛ̄ⲟⲩⲉⲡⲓⲑⲩⲙⲓⲁ
      ⲁⲓⲉⲡⲓⲑⲩⲙⲉⲓ 'I have earnestly desired' (Lk. 22.15), lit. 'with a
      desire I have desired'.

  c) ⲉ- , usually to express aim or purpose, exx. ⲧⲛ̄ϣⲟϫⲛⲉ ⲉϥⲓⲧⲟⲩ
      'we intend to remove them' (Sh. 42.38.23); ⲁⲩⲃⲱⲕ ⲇⲉ ⲉⲛⲁⲩ 'they
      went to see' (Cha. 3.22); ⲙ̄ⲡⲉϥⲟⲩⲱϣ ⲉϫⲓ 'he did not wish to receive'
      (Cha. 6.15); ⲛⲉⲧⲃⲏⲕ ⲉϩⲣⲁⲓ ⲉⲟⲩⲱϣⲧ̄ 'those who went up to worship' (Jo.
      12.20).

  d) less commonly ⲛ̄- can precede the infinitive. This construction is
      found particularly after the verbs ⲁⲣⲭⲉⲓ 'to begin' and ⲙ̄ⲡϣⲁ 'to
      be worthy', exx. ⲁϥⲁⲣⲭⲉⲓ ⲛ̄ϯⲉⲟⲟⲩ 'he began to glorify' (Cha. 31.33);
      ⲡⲁⲓ ⲉⲛϯⲙ̄ⲡϣⲁ ⲁⲛ ⲛ̄ⲃⲱⲗ ⲉⲃⲟⲗ 'this one who is unworthy to loosen
      (his sandals)' (Acts 13.25).

      It can also, though not invariably, be found after the verbs ⲙⲉ
      'to love' and ⲥⲟⲟⲩⲛ 'to know'.

e) after the verb ϣⲓⲛⲉ 'to seek', the infinitive is introduced by
ⲛ̄ⲥⲁ- , e.g. ⲉϥϣⲓⲛⲉ ⲛ̄ⲥⲁ ⲁⲙⲁϩⲧⲉ ⲙ̄ⲙⲟϥ 'seeking to lay hold of
him' (Mt. 21.46).

82 The Causative Infinitive

The causative prefixes take the following forms:

Sing. 1	ⲧⲣⲁ-	Pl.1	ⲧⲣⲉⲛ-	
2m	ⲧⲣⲉⲕ-			
2f	ⲧⲣⲉ-	2	ⲧⲣⲉⲧⲉⲧⲛ̄-	Negation: see below
3m	ⲧⲣⲉϥ-			
3f	ⲧⲣⲉⲥ-	3	ⲧⲣⲉⲩ-	

Before nom. subject ⲧⲣⲉ-

83 Like the simple infinitive, the causative can be preceded by a variety
of prefixes:

a) it can be treated as a noun and thus take an article, possessive,
or demonstrative, e.g. ⲡⲉⲓⲧⲣⲉⲧⲛ̄ ⲗⲩⲡⲓ 'this causing you to grieve'
(2 Cor. 7.11).

b) when preceded by a verbal prefix a number of permutations are
possible, depending on whether the subject and object are nouns
or pronouns:

  i) 'He caused the man to go'   ⲁϥ-ⲧⲣⲉ-ⲡⲣⲱⲙⲉ ⲃⲱⲕ
  ii) 'He caused him to go'   ⲁϥ-ⲧⲣⲉϥ- ⲃⲱⲕ
  iii) 'The man caused him to go'   ⲁ-ⲡ-ⲣⲱⲙⲉ-ⲧⲣⲉϥ ⲃⲱⲕ
  iv) 'The man caused the man to go' ⲁ- ⲡ-ⲣⲱⲙⲉ-ⲧⲣⲉ-ⲡ-ⲣⲱⲙⲉ ⲃⲱⲕ
  exx. ⲁⲡϣⲱⲛⲉ ⲧⲣⲉ ⲛⲁⲓ ⲣ̄ⲁⲧϭⲟⲙ 'the sickness has caused these to
  become powerless' (Cha. 8.10); ϣⲁⲩⲧⲣⲉⲛ†ϩⲁⲡ 'they cause us to
  sit in judgement' (Besa 97.5); ⲁⲕⲧⲣⲉⲛⲥⲟⲩⲱⲛⲅ̄ 'thou hast caused
  us to know thee' (Sh. 42.90.16).

c) ⲉ- , with the meaning 'that ..... should/might', exx. ⲁϥⲡⲁⲣⲁⲕⲁⲗⲉⲓ
ⲙ̄ⲙⲟⲟⲩ ⲉⲧⲣⲉⲩ ϣⲗⲏⲗ 'he entreated them that they might pray' (Cha.
20.16); ϥⲟⲩⲱϣ ⲉⲧⲣⲉⲛⲃⲱⲕ ϣⲁⲣⲟϥ 'he wishes that we should go unto
him' (Sh. 73.2.4); ⲉⲩⲟⲩⲱϣ ⲉⲧⲣⲉⲛⲁⲡⲟⲗⲟⲙⲓⲍⲉ ⲛⲁⲩ 'wishing that we
might make a defence for them' (Sh. 42.30.12).

d) ⲙⲛ̄ⲛ̄ⲥⲁ-, giving the meaning 'after ....', exx. ⲙⲛ̄ⲛ̄ⲥⲁⲧⲣⲉⲩⲃⲱⲕ ⲉⲃⲟⲗ
ϩⲓⲧⲟⲟⲧⲛ̄ 'after they had left us' (Sh. 42.129.9); ⲙⲛ̄ⲛ̄ⲥⲁⲧⲣⲉⲥ ⲙⲟⲩ

'after she had died' (Cha. 55.22); ⲙⲛ̄ⲛ̄ⲥⲁⲧⲣⲉⲕϯⲥⲃⲱ ⲛⲁⲩ 'after thou hast taught them' (Sh. 42.169.12).

e) ϩⲙ̄ⲡ- (preposition ϩⲛ̄ + definite article), usually with temporal meaning — 'when/while/as .... was/is happening', though occasionally it has a different usage, e.g. 'by means of', exx. ϩⲙ̄ⲡⲣⲉⲩⲉⲓ ⲉⲃⲟⲗ ϩⲛ̄ⲧⲙⲉⲥⲟⲡⲟⲧⲁⲙⲓⲁ 'when he was coming out of Mesopotamia' (Sh. 42.100.15); ϩⲙ̄ⲡⲧⲣⲉ ⲡⲉⲧⲛ̄ϩⲏⲧ ⲛ̄ⲁⲧⲥⲃⲱ ⲣ̄-ⲕⲁⲕⲉ 'when your ignorant heart was darkened' (Besa 73.13); ϩⲙ̄ⲡⲣⲉⲩ ϩⲁⲣⲉϩ ⲉⲛⲉⲕϣⲁϫⲉ '(wherewith shall a young man straighten his way) By keeping your words' (Besa 76.29).

f) ⲛ̄ⲥⲁ- , a rather uncommon construction which gives the meaning 'except, unless ...', e.g. ⲙⲛ̄ ϭⲉ ⲟⲣⲅⲏ ⲛ̄ⲥⲁⲧⲣⲉ ⲡⲛⲟⲩⲧⲉ ⲥϩⲟⲩⲣ ⲡⲣⲱⲙⲉ ⲛ̄ⲕⲣⲟⲩ 'there is no anger beyond God cursing deceitful man' (Sh. 42.189.6).

g) ϩⲱⲥⲧⲉ ⲉ- ; this construction is used as a variant of ⲉⲧⲣⲉ- (c above) with the same meaning of 'that ..... should/might happen', e.g. ϩⲱⲥⲧⲉ ⲉⲧⲣⲁϣⲱⲡⲉ ⲛ̄ⲑⲉ ⲛ̄ⲟⲩⲡⲟⲛⲏⲣⲟⲥ 'so that I should be like a wicked man' (Besa 118.35).

h) ⲙ̄ⲡⲣ- , as negation of the Optative (§ 66).

84 Both forms of the infinitive are negated by ⲧⲙ̄ . With the simple infinitive ⲧⲙ̄ stands immediately before the verb, while with the causative infinitive it normally stands before the causative element ⲧⲣⲉ- , exx. ⲉⲧⲙ̄ⲣⲓⲙⲉ 'not to weep' (Sh. 42.95.8); ⲕⲟⲩⲱϣ ⲉⲧⲙ̄ⲧⲣⲁ ⲩⲉⲓ ⲣⲟⲟⲩϣ 'do you wish that I should not bother?' (Cha. 5.21); ⲉⲧⲙ̄ⲱϣ ⲉⲃⲟⲗ 'not to call out' (Sh. 73.68.11). But with ϩⲙ̄ⲡⲧⲣⲉ ⲧⲙ̄ follows the causative element, e.g. ϩⲙ̄ⲡⲧⲣⲁⲧⲙ̄ϭⲛ̄ ϩⲱⲃ 'when I do not find work' (Cha. 10.17).

85 To express 'to be able to ....' (with negative 'unable'), the verb (ⲉ)ϣ- 'be able' is attached to the required infinitive, exx. ⲛ̄ⲧⲛ̄ⲛⲁ ϣϭⲟⲧⲡⲟⲩ ⲁⲛ ⲉⲃⲟⲗ ⲙ̄ⲡⲛⲟⲩⲧⲉ 'we shall not be able to scare them away from God' (Sh. 42.167.25); ⲛ̄ⲁϣ ⲛ̄ϩⲉ ⲛ̄ⲧⲱⲧⲛ̄ ⲉⲧⲉⲧⲛⲁ ϣⲡⲓⲥⲧⲉⲩⲉ 'how will you be able to believe?' (Jo. 5.44).

XI THE PASSIVE (T. §§ 255, 326)

86   Often the infinitives of verbs can have passive as well as active meaning, e.g. ⲧⲁⲕⲟ 'to destroy' or 'to be destroyed'. Normally, however,
the passive is expressed in a rather roundabout manner. 'The man was
found' would be rendered as 'they found the man', 'he was found' as
'they found him', i.e. the 3rd person plural is utilised, exx. ⲁⲩⲧⲁⲙⲟⲛ
'we have been told' (Besa 98.9); ⲛⲧⲉⲣⲟⲩϫⲛⲟⲩⲕ   'when you were asked'
(Besa 24.30). The agent, i.e. 'he was found by the man', is normally
expressed by ϩⲓⲧⲛ- , exx. ⲛⲥⲉⲙⲉⲥⲧⲱⲟⲩ ⲉⲃⲟⲗ ϩⲓⲧⲙⲡⲛⲟⲩⲧⲉ 'and they are
hated by God' (Besa 34.29); ⲁⲩⲧⲁⲙⲟⲛ ⲉⲡⲁⲓ ϩⲓⲧⲙⲡⲉ ⲯⲁⲗⲙⲱⲇⲟⲥ 'we were
told this by the psalmist' (Besa 76.27).

XII PREPOSITIONS

87   Below is a list of the commonest prepositions and their basic meanings.
A more comprehensive list will be found in Plumley, op. cit., p. 122ff.,
but the full range of meanings is best acquired by reference to Crum's
dictionary. The nominal forms of the prepositions are given first
followed by the pronominal, which take the suffix pronouns.

a) ⲉ-, ⲉⲣⲟ⸗ (Crum 50a); 'to, towards, for, from, in order to'. Also
used to express comparison, e.g. ⲡⲉⲧϫⲟⲟⲣ ⲉⲣⲟⲓ 'the one who is stronger than me' (Mk. 1.7).

b) ⲛ-, ⲙⲙⲟ⸗ (C. 215a); 'with (instrument), in (temporal or local),
to, from'

c) ⲛ-, ⲛⲁ⸗ (C. 216a); dative 'to, for'; before the 2nd plural
suffix ⲛⲏ⸗

d) ⲙⲛ-, ⲛⲙⲙⲁ⸗ (C. 169b); '(together) with'; before the 2nd person
plural suffix ⲛⲙⲙⲏ⸗

e) ϣⲁ-, ϣⲁⲣⲟ⸗ (C. 541b); 'towards' (normally of people), 'until'

f) ϩⲓ-, ϩⲓ(ⲱ)ⲱ⸗ (C. 643b); 'on, at, in the time of'

g) ϩⲁ-, ϩⲁⲣⲟ⸗ (C. 632a); 'under, in, at, by reason of'

h) ϩⲛ-, ⲛϩⲏⲧ⸗ (C. 683a); 'in' (temporal or local), 'by (agent)';
preceded by ⲉⲃⲟⲗ 'out of, from', e.g. ⲟⲩⲁ ⲉⲃⲟⲗ ⲛϩⲏⲧⲧⲏⲩⲧⲛ
'one of you'

i) ⲉⲝⲛ̄-, ⲉⲭⲱ= (C. 757a); 'upon, over'

j) ⲛ̄ⲥⲁ-, ⲛ̄ⲥⲱ= (C. 314a); 'behind, after'

k) ⲉⲧⲃⲉ-, ⲉⲧⲃⲏⲏⲧ= (C. 61a); 'because of, concerning, for the sake of'

l) ϩⲓⲭⲛ̄-, ϩⲓⲭⲱ= (C. 758b); 'upon, over'

m) ⲉⲣⲁⲧ= (C. 303a); 'to' (of people)

n) ⲛ̄ⲧⲛ̄-, ⲛ̄ⲧⲟⲟⲧ= (C. 427b); 'in, by, beside, from, with'; before 2nd person plural suffix ⲛ̄ⲧⲉ=

o) ⲙ̄ⲡⲉⲙⲧⲟ (C. 193a); from ⲙ̄ⲧⲟ ; always taking a definite article or possessive adjective in agreement with the subject, and always followed by ⲉⲃⲟⲗ , with the meaning 'before' (local), exx. ⲙ̄ⲡⲉⲕⲙ̄ⲧⲟ ⲉⲃⲟⲗ 'before you' (Mt. 11.10); ⲙ̄ⲡⲉⲙⲧⲟ ⲉⲃⲟⲗ ⲙ̄ⲡⲙⲏⲏϣⲉ 'before the multitude' (Mt. 27.24)

p) ϩⲓⲧⲛ̄-, ϩⲓⲧⲟⲟⲧ= (C. 428b); 'through, by, from'

q) ϩⲁϩⲧⲛ̄-, ϩⲁ(ϩ)ⲧⲏ= (C. 717a); 'with, beside'

EXERCISE V
Vocabulary

ⲁⲓⲥⲑⲁⲛⲉ Perceive, realise

ⲉⲓⲱ, ⲉⲓⲁ-, ⲉⲓⲁⲁ=, ⲉⲓⲏ⁺ Wash

ⲕⲱⲗⲅⲉ To hinder

ⲕⲱⲛⲥ̄, ⲕⲉⲛⲥ̄-, ⲕⲟ(ⲟ)ⲛⲥ̄=, ⲕⲟⲛⲥ̄⁺ Slay, pierce

ⲕⲱⲧ, ⲕⲉⲧ-, ⲕⲟⲧ=, ⲕⲏⲩ⁺ Build, form

ⲕ̄ⲧⲟ, ⲕ̄ⲧⲉ-, ⲕ̄ⲧⲟ=, ⲕ̄ⲧⲏⲩ⁺ Turn, surround; return (usually reflexive) (C. 127b)

ⲗⲟ Cease, stop + ϩⲛ̄- Cease from (C. 135a)

ⲙ̄ⲕⲁϩ, ⲙⲟⲕϩ̄⁺ ; Painful, difficult; be grieved. Also m. noun – Pain, grief

ⲙⲉⲩⲉ Think; m. noun – Thought ⲣ̄-ⲡⲙⲉⲉⲩⲉ Remember (C. 199a)

ⲣ̄-ⲙ̄ⲡϣⲁ Become worthy, deserve

ⲣⲓⲙⲉ Weep

ⲣⲱϣⲉ, ⲣⲉϣⲧ̄-, ⲣⲁϣⲧ̄= : Suffice; +ⲉ- Suffice for (C. 309a)

ⲣ̄-ϩⲱⲃ To work (C. 654a)

ⲥⲱⲃⲉ Laugh, mock; m. noun – laughter

ⲥⲟⲟⲩⲧⲛ̄, ⲥⲟⲩⲧⲛ̄-, ⲥⲟⲩⲧⲱⲛ=, ⲥⲟⲩⲧⲱⲛ⁺ ; be straight, upright (C. 371a)

ⲥⲱⲟⲩϩ, ⲥⲉⲩϩ-, ⲥⲟⲟⲩϩ=, ⲥⲟⲟⲩϩ⁺ ; Gather, collect (C. 372b); as m. noun – Gathering, community. A f. form is written ⲥⲟⲟⲩϩⲥ̄

ⲧⲁⲕⲟ, ⲧⲁⲕⲉ-, ⲧⲁⲕⲟ=, ⲧⲁⲕⲏⲩ (ⲧ)⁺   Destroy, perish (C. 405a)

ⲥⲟⲟⲕⲉ, ⲥⲁⲕⲉ-, ⲥⲁⲕⲱ=, ⲥⲁⲕⲏⲩ⁺   Remove (normally reflexive);
      often + ⲉⲃⲟⲗ (C. 380a)

ϯ-ⲉⲃⲟⲗ   Sell (C. 394b)

ⲟⲩⲱⲙ, ⲟⲩ(ⲉ)ⲙ-, ⲟⲩⲟⲙ=   Eat, bite

ⲟⲩⲱϣ, ⲟⲩⲉϣ-, ⲟⲩⲱϣ=   Wish, desire (C. 500a); **m. noun** will, wish

ⲟⲩⲱϩ, ⲟⲩⲉϩ-, ⲟⲩⲁϩ=, ⲟⲩⲏϩ⁺   Put, set; +ⲉ- add to; + ⲛⲥⲁ- (ⲛⲥⲱ=)
      follow (usually reflexive) C. 505b)

ϣⲱⲡ, ϣⲉⲡ-, ϣⲟⲡ=, ϣⲏⲡ⁺   Receive, take (C. 574b)

ϣ̄ϣⲉ   To be fitting, right; (usually + ⲉ- (ⲉⲣⲟ=), fitting for ...)

ϩⲟⲙⲟⲗⲟⲅⲉⲓ   To confess

ϫⲓ, ϫⲓ-, ϫⲓⲧ=, ϫⲏⲩ⁺   Take, receive (C. 747b)

ϫⲛⲟⲩ, ϫⲛⲉⲧ, ϫⲛⲟⲩ=   Ask, question (C. 774a)

ϭⲉⲡⲏ   Hasten; ϩⲛⲟⲩϭⲉⲡⲏ Quickly

ϭⲙ̄ -   (+ article or possessive)-ϣⲓⲛⲉ   Visit

ⲉⲡⲓⲑⲩⲙⲓⲁ	Desire, lust (f)	ϩⲟⲩⲟ	Great part (m)
ⲏ	Or; ⲏ ....ⲏ Either .... or	ⲉϩⲟⲩⲟ ⲉ-	more than;
ⲙⲁⲅⲉⲓⲣⲟⲥ	Cook (m)	ⲛ̄ϩⲟⲩⲟ	greatly, very,
ⲙⲁⲅⲟⲥ	Magi		especially (C. 735a)
ⲙⲏⲏϣⲉ	Multitude (m)	ϭⲟⲙ	Power, strength (f);
ⲥⲡⲩⲗⲁⲓⲟⲛ	Cave, hole (m)	ϭⲙ̄ϭⲟⲙ	Be able, strong
ⲥⲁⲧⲁⲛⲁⲥ	Satan		(similar (ⲉ)ϣϭⲙ̄ϭⲟⲙ)
ⲟⲩⲉⲣⲏⲧⲉ	Foot (f)		(C. 815b)
ϩⲛⲟⲩϣⲉ̄ⲛⲉ	At a moment, suddenly		
	(from ϣⲉ̄ⲛⲉ)		

A English into Coptic

1 You do not wish to come unto me

2 Their going in and their going out

3 He began to wash the feet of his disciples

4 Do it quickly

5 I will cause your heart to grieve

6 After he had received the bread, Satan entered into him

7 An old man was asked

8 It was said concerning one of the brethren

9 When you transgressed the commandment

10 You have caused us to be worthy

11 When this great multitude gathered here

12 We did not realise that we should depart

13 Especially that we should not destroy our body

14 Let us be careful not to defile

15 Neither to eat nor drink for (ⲛ̄-) two days

16 To build or not to build, to eat or not to eat

B Coptic into English

1 ϣ̄ϣⲉ ⲉⲣⲟⲩ ⲉⲙⲟⲩ

2 ϣⲁⲩⲧⲣⲉⲛ ⲥⲱⲃⲉ ϩ̄ⲙ̄ⲡⲥⲏⲩ ⲛ̄ⲣⲓⲙⲉ ⲁⲩⲱ ϣⲁⲩⲧⲣⲉⲛⲣⲓⲙⲉ ϩ̄ⲙ̄ⲡⲥⲏⲩ ⲛ̄ⲥⲱⲃⲉ

3 ⲁⲩⲥⲱⲃⲉ ⲙ̄ⲙⲟⲩ ⲉⲃⲟⲗ ϩⲓⲧ̄ⲛ̄ ⲙ̄ⲙⲁⲅⲟⲥ

4 ⲩ̄ⲛⲁⲧⲁⲕⲟ ϩ̄ⲛⲟⲩ ϣϭ̄ⲛⲉ

5 ⲙ̄ⲡ̄ⲛ̄ ⲟⲩⲁϩ̄ⲛ̄ ⲛ̄ⲥⲁ ⲡⲛⲟⲩⲧⲉ ϩ̄ⲛⲟⲩⲥⲟⲟⲩⲧ̄ⲛ̄ ⲉⲧⲣⲉⲛⲥⲟⲩⲛ ⲧⲉϩⲓⲏ ⲙ̄ⲡ̄ⲭⲟⲉⲓⲥ

6 ⲕ̄ⲧⲣⲉ ⲛⲉⲕ ⲙⲁⲅⲉⲓⲣⲟⲥ ⲣ̄-ϩⲱⲃ ⲛⲁⲕ

7 ⲙⲛ̄ⲛ̄ⲥⲁⲧⲣⲉⲩⲧⲱⲟⲩⲛ ϩ̄ⲙ̄ⲡⲙⲁ ⲛ̄ⲟⲩⲱⲙ ⲙ̄ⲡⲟⲩ ⲉϣϭ̄ⲙϭⲟⲙ ⲉⲟⲩⲱⲙ ⲙ̄ⲡⲉⲩⲟⲉⲓⲕ

8 ⲛ̄ⲛⲉⲥ ϣⲱⲡⲉ ⲉⲧⲣⲁ ⲣ̄-ⲛⲟⲃⲉ ⲙ̄ⲡⲉⲙⲧⲟ ⲉⲃⲟⲗ ⲙ̄ⲡ̄ⲭⲟⲉⲓⲥ

9 ⲙ̄ⲙ̄ⲛ̄ ⲗⲁⲁⲩ ⲛⲁϣϭ̄ⲙϭⲟⲙ ⲉⲕⲱⲗⲅⲉ ⲙ̄ⲙⲟⲟⲩ

10 ⲛ̄ⲛⲉⲩ ϣ̄ⲉⲓ ϣⲁⲣⲟⲟⲩ ⲉⲧⲣⲉⲩϭ̄ⲙⲡⲉⲩ ϣⲓⲛⲉ

11 ϣ̄ϣⲉ ⲟⲛ ⲉⲧⲙ̄ϯ ⲉⲃⲟⲗ

12 ϣⲁⲛⲧⲉⲩⲧⲣⲉⲩ ϩⲟⲙⲟⲗⲟⲅⲉⲓ ⲛ̄ⲛⲉⲩⲙⲉⲉⲩⲉ

13 ϩ̄ⲙ̄ⲡⲧⲣⲉⲛ ⲕⲧⲟⲛ ⲁⲛⲉⲓ ⲉϫⲙ̄ⲡⲉⲥⲡⲩⲗⲁⲓⲟⲛ ⲉⲧ̄ⲙ̄ⲙⲁⲩ

14 ⲛ̄ⲧⲁⲩⲧⲁⲁⲩ ⲙ̄ⲡⲛⲟⲩⲧⲉ

15 ⲟⲩⲛⲧ̄ⲉ̄ ⲧⲉϩⲟⲩⲥⲓⲁ ⲉⲕⲱⲛ̄ⲉ̄ ⲏ ⲉⲧ̄ⲙ̄ⲕⲱⲛ̄ⲉ̄

16 ⲁⲩ ⲗⲟ ϩ̄ⲙ̄ⲡⲛⲟⲃⲉ ⲉⲧ̄ⲙ̄ⲧⲣⲉⲩ ϣⲱⲡⲉ ϩ̄ⲛ̄- ⲛ̄ⲉⲡⲓⲑⲩⲙⲓⲁ ⲛ̄ⲛ̄ⲣⲱⲙⲉ

XIII   THE VERBAL SENTENCE

88   Word Order (T. § 378ff)

The normal word order is:

VERBAL PREFIX, SUBJECT (nominal or pronominal), VERB, OBJECT (nominal or pronominal), DATIVE, ADVERB

There are a number of circumstances in which this word order can be upset.

89   A pronominal dative (ⲉⲣⲟ⸗ and ⲛ̄ⲥⲱ⸗ also) precedes a <u>nominal</u> object, which is then introduced by ⲛ̄- , exx. ⲁⲩϯ ⲛⲁⲩ ⲛ̄ⲧⲉⲍⲟⲩⲥⲓⲁ   'he gave them the power' (Jo. 1.12); ⲙ̄ⲡⲉϥⲟⲩⲱⲛ ⲛⲁϥ ⲙ̄ⲡⲣⲟ   'he did not open the door unto him' (Cha. 34.7); ⲉⲁⲩⲕⲱⲧ ⲛⲁⲩ ⲛ̄ϩⲉⲛⲏⲓ   'having built houses for themselves' (Sh. 42.96.20).

90   The word order can often be upset by a desire to emphasise a particular element in the sentence.

  a)   a <u>nominal subject</u> can be emphasised by placing it at the head of the sentence, but it must then be reiterated by means of the pronominal forms of the prefix conjugation, exx. ⲁⲛⲧⲱⲛⲓⲟⲥ ⲇⲉ ⲁϥϣⲡ̄ϩⲙⲟⲧ   'Anthony gave thanks' (St. A. 10.4); ⲛ̄ⲓⲟⲩⲇⲁⲓ ϭⲉ ⲛⲉⲩⲙⲓϣⲉ   'therefore the Jews were contending' (Jo. 6.52); ⲓ̄ⲥ ⲇⲉ ⲁϥⲁϣⲕⲁⲕ   'and Jesus cried out' (Jo. 7.28).

  b)   a <u>pronominal subject</u> is stressed by placing an independent pronoun at the beginning of the sentence, followed by the prefix conjugation, exx. ⲁⲛⲟⲕ ϯⲛⲁⲧⲟⲩⲛⲟⲥϥ̄   'I shall raise him up' (Jo. 6.40); ⲁⲛⲟⲛ ⲁⲛⲡⲓⲥⲧⲉⲩⲉ   'we believed' (Jo. 6.69).

91   When the subject is nominal this is often referred to at the beginning of the sentence by means of the pronominal forms of the prefix conjugation, and is then identified specifically later in the sentence by the use of ⲛ̄ϭⲓ, 'namely', exx. ⲛ̄ⲧⲉⲣⲉϥⲛⲁⲩ ⲉⲣⲟϥ ⲛ̄ϭⲓ ⲁⲛⲧⲱⲛⲓⲟⲥ   'when he had seen him, namely Anthony' (St. A. 5.13); ⲁⲩⲥⲱⲧⲙ̄ ⲛ̄ϭⲓ ⲛ̄ϣⲏⲣⲉ ⲙ̄ⲡⲓ̄ⲏ̄ⲗ 'they heard, namely the children of Israel' (Besa 61.22); ⲥⲉⲥϩⲟⲩⲟⲣⲧ̄ ⲉⲡⲉϩⲟⲩⲟ ⲛ̄ⲛⲁϩⲣⲙ̄ⲡⲛⲟⲩⲧⲉ ⲙⲛ̄ⲛ̄ⲣⲱⲙⲉ ⲛ̄ϭⲓ ⲛⲉⲧⲉⲓⲣⲉ ⲛ̄ⲛⲁⲓ   'they are cursed all the more before God and men, namely those who do these things' (Besa 69.14).

In order to avoid a clumsy translation it is best to render passages
using this construction as if the subject was, in fact, only men-
tioned once, i.e. 'When Anthony had seen him', 'the children of
Israel heard', etc. As the above examples indicate, ⲚϬⲓ can be
employed whether the subject consists of one or several words, and
for this reason would appear to be purely a stylistic gloss. However, it is a useful method to remember when translating <u>into</u> Coptic
and the subject is particularly long, when the verbal prefix and the
verb would otherwise be separated by several words.

92 c) <u>The object,</u> whether nominal or pronominal, can be emphasised in
the same way as the subject, i.e. by placing it at the head of
the sentence and reiterating it pronominally, exx. ⲠⲘⲟⲟⲨ
ⲉⲩϢⲁⲛⲧⲁ₂ϥ 'if the water is mixed' (Sh. 42.52.6); ⲚⲁⲤⲁⲂⲂⲁⲧⲟⲛ
ⲉⲧⲉⲧⲛⲉ₂ⲁⲣⲉ₂ ⲉⲣⲟⲟⲩ 'you shall keep my Sabbaths' (Sh. 42.96.1).

93 The object can be <u>direct,</u> i.e. immediately following the verb,
or <u>indirect,</u> when it is introduced by Ⲛ- (ⲘⲘⲟ= before pronominal
objects) or, in some cases, by Ⲉ- (Ⲉⲣⲟ=) – see below § 94. An
important rule applies here:

With the <u>1st Present, 2nd Present, Circumstantial Present</u> and
<u>Imperfect</u> tenses THE OBJECT IS ALWAYS INDIRECT, and the preceding
verb <u>must</u> take the ABSOLUTE form (§ 50a), exx. ⲚⲉⲨⲤⲱⲕ ⲘⲘⲟⲛ
'they were inciting us' (Sh. 42.30.14); ϯⲧⲁⲉⲓⲟ ⲘⲠⲁⲉⲓⲱⲧ 'I
honour my Father' (Jo. 8.49); Ⲡⲁⲉⲓⲱⲧ Ⲙⲉ ⲘⲘⲟⲓ 'my Father loves
me' (Jo. 10.17); ϯⲤⲟⲟⲨⲛ ⲘⲠⲉⲓⲱⲧ 'I know the Father' (Jo. 10.15);
ⲚⲉⲨⲣⲱϢⲉ ⲘⲘⲟⲛ ⲁⲛ 'they did not suffice us' (Cha. 55.2).

The only exception to this rule is the verb ⲟⲨⲱϢ 'wish', which
always takes a direct object.

With other tenses either the direct or indirect method can be
employed, the direct more commonly. If the object is <u>direct</u> the
verbs takes the CONSTRUCT form when the object is nominal and
the PRONOMINAL form if it is pronominal, exx. ⲁⲩⲧⲁⲙⲉ Ⲛⲓⲟⲩⲇⲁⲓ
'he told the Jews' (Jo. 5.15); ⲁⲓϪⲛⲟⲩϥ 'I asked him' (Sh. 42.
38.17); ⲁⲩϪⲓⲧϥ ...... ⲁⲩⲧⲁⲁⲥ ⲛⲁⲩ 'he took him, ... he gave

it to him' (Cha. 6.14); ⲁϥϭⲓⲛⲉ ⲛ̄ⲧⲉϥⲙⲁⲁⲩ   'he found his mother' (Cha. 1.6); ⲙⲉϥϭⲛ̄ ⲙⲁⲛⲟⲩⲱϩ   'he finds no dwelling-place' (Cha. 15.9).

94 Some verbs normally have their object introduced by ⲉ- (ⲉⲣⲟ≠), though most of these can also take ⲛ̄- . They include the following common verbs:

ⲛⲁⲩ 'see'; ⲉⲓⲙⲉ 'know'; ⲙⲉⲉⲩⲉ 'think'; ⲥⲱⲧⲙ̄ 'hear'; ⲙⲟⲩⲧⲉ 'call'; ⲥⲙⲟⲩ 'bless'; ϩⲁⲣⲉϩ 'keep'; ϣⲓⲛⲉ 'greet'; ⲣ̄-ϩⲟⲧⲉ 'fear'; ϩⲉ 'find'; ⲥⲁϩⲟⲩ 'curse'; ⲡⲓⲥⲧⲉⲩⲉ 'believe'

exx. ⲁⲩⲛⲁⲩ ⲉⲛ̄ϩⲗ̄ⲗⲟ   'they saw the old men' (Cha. 15.16); ⲁⲩⲥⲱⲧⲙ̄ ⲉⲡϣⲁϫⲉ   'he heard the word' (Cha. 18.3); ⲡϫⲟⲉⲓⲥ ⲅⲁⲣ ⲙⲟⲩⲧⲉ ⲉⲣⲟⲛ   'for the Lord calls us' (Besa 51.20).

95 Note that the verb ϫⲱ 'say' must <u>always</u> take an object, i.e. ϥ̄ϫⲱ ⲙ̄ⲙⲟⲥ 'he says it' (indirect object) or ⲁϥϫⲟⲟⲥ 'he said it' (direct object). 'It', however, is not rendered in the translation. (This rule does not apply to ⲡⲉϫⲉ- , ⲡⲉϫⲁ≠).

Greek verbs take the indirect object.

96 d) The usual method of emphasising an <u>adverb</u> is to employ a second tense. Sometimes, however, adverbial expressions stand at the beginning of the sentence, especially expressions of time, exx. ⲙⲛ̄ⲛⲥⲁ ⲟⲩⲟⲉⲓϣ ⲇⲉ ⲁϥϣⲱⲛⲉ   'after a time he became sick' (Cha. 1.4); ϫⲓⲛ ⲡⲉϩⲟⲟⲩ ⲉⲧⲙ̄ⲙⲁⲩ ⲁⲩϫⲓϣⲟϫⲛⲉ   'from that day they took counsel' (Jo. 11.53); ⲙⲛ̄ⲛⲥⲱⲥ ⲁϥϫⲟⲟⲣⲟⲩ ⲉⲃⲟⲗ 'afterwards he dispersed them' (Sh. 42.99.19).

97 <u>Speech</u>

Both direct and indirect speech are introduced by the particle ϫⲉ. With direct speech this is left untranslated. With indirect speech it can often be rendered as 'that'. When introducing questions it sometimes has the meaning 'whether', exx. ⲡⲉϫⲁϥ ⲇⲉ ⲛⲁϥ ⲛ̄ϭⲓ ⲡⲣ̄ⲣⲟ ϫⲉ ⲕ̄ⲥⲟⲟⲩⲛ ϫⲉ ⲁⲛⲅ̄ ⲛⲓⲙ   'the king said to him: 'do you know who I am?'' (Cha. 31.26); ⲧⲉⲧⲛ̄ⲙⲟⲩⲧⲉ ⲉⲣⲟⲓ ϫⲉ ⲡⲥⲁϩ ⲁⲩⲱ ⲡϫⲟⲉⲓⲥ 'you call me teacher and Lord' (Jo. 13.13).

Vocabulary

ⲙⲟⲥⲧⲉ , ⲙⲉⲥⲧⲉ- , ⲙⲉⲥⲧⲱ⸗ Hate; ⲙⲟⲥⲧⲉ Hatred (m) (C. 187a)

ⲙⲟⲩⲍ , ⲙⲉⲍ- , ⲙⲁⲍ⸗ , ⲙⲏⲍ⁺ Fill (C. 208a)

ⲥⲍⲁⲓ , ⲥⲉⲍ- , ⲥⲁⲍ⸗ , ⲥⲏⲍ⁺ Write (C. 381b – see Crum for variant forms)

ⲧⲱⲃⲍ̄ , ⲧⲃⲍ̄- , ⲧⲟⲃⲍ̄⸗ Pray, entreat

ⲱϣ , ⲉϣ- , ⲟϣ⸗ Cry, announce, read; + ⲉⲃⲟⲗ Cry out (C. 533a)

ϥⲓ , ϥⲓ- , ϥⲓⲧ⸗ Bear, carry, take, lift; + ⲉⲃⲟⲗ Take away; + ⲉⲍⲣⲁⲓ
    Lift up (C. 620a)

ϣⲟⲧⲍ̄ , ϣⲉⲧⲍ(ⲉ)ⲧ- , ϣⲉⲧϩⲱⲧ⸗ , ϣⲉⲧϩⲱⲧ⁺ Inquire, examine; <u>m. noun</u> Question

ϭⲱⲗⲡ̄ , ϭ(ⲉ)ⲗⲡ̄- , ϭⲟⲗⲡ̄⸗ , ϭⲟⲗⲡ̄⁺ Uncover, reveal, open; often followed by ⲉⲃⲟⲗ
    (C. 812a)

ⲁⲣⲭⲓⲉⲣⲉⲩⲉ	High-Priest	ⲥⲱⲛⲉ	Sister
ⲃⲁⲡⲧⲓⲥⲙⲁ	Baptism (m);	ⲥⲫⲟⲥ	Cross (m)
ⲃⲁⲡⲧⲓⲍⲉ	Baptize	ⲧⲉⲛⲟⲩ	Now
ⲇⲉⲓⲡⲛⲟⲛ	Supper (m) (or Meal)	ⲧⲓⲧⲗⲟⲥ	Title (m)
ⲉⲟⲟⲩ Glory; ϯ-ⲉⲟⲟⲩ Glorify (C. 62a)		ⲭⲓⲛ	From, since (C. 772b)
ⲕⲏⲫⲁⲥ	Kephas	ⲟⲩⲇⲉ	Or
ⲕⲟⲧ	Basket (C. 127a)	ϭⲓⲭ	Hand (f)
ⲙⲩⲥⲧⲏⲣⲓⲟⲛ	Mystery (m)		
ⲡⲓⲗⲁⲧⲟⲥ	Pilate		

A <u>English into Coptic</u>

1 The Father loves the Son, and he has given all things (in)to his hands

2 He entreated God, saying: 'O Lord, reveal to me this mystery'

3 <u>In that day</u> you will ask in my name

4 They made him a supper in that place

5 They were thine, and thou hast given them to me, and they have kept thy word

6 His mother and his mother's sister were standing by the cross of Jesus

7 <u>I</u> have given them the glory

58

8 They gathered them (in), and they filled twelve baskets

9 <u>Because of this,</u> let us repent

10 Now, they have seen me, they have hated me and my Father also

B <u>Coptic into English</u>

1 ⲚⲦⲟⲕ ⲈⲨⲈⲘⲟⲨⲦⲈ Ⲉⲣⲟⲕ ⲬⲈ ⲔⲎ ⲫⲁⲥ

2 ⲀⲚⲟⲕ Ⲁⲓϯ ⲚⲀⲨ ⲘⲠⲈⲔϢⲀⲬⲈ ⲀⲨⲰ ⲠⲔⲟⲤⲘⲟⲤ ⲀⲨⲘⲈⲤⲦⲰⲟⲨ

3 ⲘⲠⲟⲨⲤⲟⲨⲚ ⲠⲀⲈⲓⲰⲦ ⲟⲨⲆⲈ ⲘⲠⲟⲨⲤⲟⲨⲰⲚϤ

4 ⲠⲈⲓⲦⲓⲦⲗⲟⲥ ϬⲈ Ⲁ ϨⲀϨ ⲚⲚⲓⲟⲨⲆⲀⲓ ⲟϢϤ

5 ⲚⲈⲨⲬⲰ ⲘⲘⲟⲥ ⲚⲀⲨ ⲚϬⲓ ⲚⲔⲈⲘⲀⲐⲎⲦⲎⲤ ⲬⲈ ⲀⲚⲚⲀⲨ ⲈⲠⲬⲟⲈⲓⲤ

6 ⲬⲓⲚ ⲦⲈⲨⲚⲟⲨ ⲈⲦⲘⲘⲀⲨ ⲀⲠⲘⲀⲐⲎⲦⲎⲤ ⲬⲓⲦϤ ⲈϨⲟⲨⲚ ⲈⲠⲈϤⲎⲓ

7 ⲀⲚⲟⲚ ϨⲰⲰⲚ ⲀⲨϯ ⲚⲀⲚ ⲘⲠⲂⲀⲠⲦⲓⲤⲘⲀ

8 ⲀⲨⲀⲣⲬⲈⲓ ⲚϬⲓ ⲠⲢⲢⲟ ⲚϨⲟⲦϨ̄Ⲧ ⲘⲘⲟⲨ ⲈⲨⲬⲰ ⲘⲘⲟⲥ

9 ⲚⲀⲓ ⲀⲨⲬⲟⲟⲨ ⲚϬⲓ Ⲓ̄Ⲥ ⲀⲨϤⲓ ⲚⲈⲨⲂⲀⲗ ⲈϨⲣⲀⲓ ⲈⲦⲠⲈ ⲈⲨⲬⲰ ⲘⲘⲟⲥ ⲬⲈ
   ⲠⲀⲈⲓⲰⲦ, ⲀⲦⲈⲨⲚⲟⲨ Ⲉⲓ

10 ⲚⲈⲨⲬⲰ ⲘⲘⲟⲥ ⲘⲠⲓⲗⲀⲦⲟⲥ ⲚϬⲓ ⲚⲀⲢⲬⲓⲈⲣⲈⲨⲈ ⲚⲚⲓⲟⲨⲆⲀⲓ ⲬⲈ ⲘⲠⲢⲤⲀϨϤ
   ⲬⲈ ⲠⲢ̄Ⲣⲟ ⲚⲚⲓⲟⲨⲆⲀⲓ

XIV <u>QUESTIONS</u> (T. § 430ff)

98 A When an interrogative word ('who?', 'what?', 'which?', etc)
   is present, one of the following interrogative pronouns or
   adverbs is used:

   (a) ⲦⲰⲚ 'where?'; (b) ⲈⲂⲟⲗ ⲦⲰⲚ 'whence?'; (c) ⲈⲦⲰⲚ
   'whither?'; (d) ⲈⲦⲂⲈ ⲟⲨ 'why?'; (e) ⲀϨⲣⲟ= 'why?' – always
   taking a suffix in agreement with the subject; (f) ϢⲀⲦⲚⲀⲨ
   'until when?', 'how long?' (this can also be expressed by using
   ϢⲀⲚⲦⲈ ⲟⲨ ϯ ϢⲰⲠⲈ ; (g) ⲚⲓⲘ 'who?', 'what?', 'which?',
   + Ⲛ̄- before a noun; (h) ⲟⲨ 'what?', + Ⲛ̄- before a noun;
   (i) ⲀϢ 'who?', 'what?', 'which?', + Ⲛ- before a noun; (j) ⲚⲀϢ Ⲛ̄ϨⲈ
   'how?'; (k) ⲦⲚ̄ⲀⲨ 'when?'; (l) ⲟⲨⲎⲣ 'how many?', 'how much?',
   'how great?', + Ⲛ̄- before a noun.

   It is possible to obtain further nuances of meaning by employing
   these interrogative pronouns and adverbs in compound phrases,

exx. ⳩ⲛⲟⲩ 'with what?', 'by what?'; ⲛ̄ⲥⲁ ⲛⲓⲙ 'except whom?', 'after whom?', etc.

99 Of the above ⲧⲱⲛ , ⲉⲃⲟⲗ ⲧⲱⲛ , ⲉⲧⲱⲛ and ⲧⲛ̄ⲁⲩ invariably appear after the verb, which must therefore <u>always take a second tense</u>, exx. ⲉⲣⲉ ⲡⲁⲓ ⲛⲁⲃⲱⲕ ⲉⲧⲱⲛ 'where will this one go?' (Jo. 7.35); ⲉⲕⲟⲩⲏ⳩ ⲧⲱⲛ 'where are you dwelling?' (Jo. 1.38); ⲛ̄ⲧⲁⲕⲃⲱⲕ ⲉⲧⲱⲛ 'whither hast thou gone?' (Besa 24.25).

But when the subject is <u>nominal</u> ⲧⲱⲛ is preceded by the relevant prefix of the 2nd Present, exx. ⲉⲩⲧⲱⲛ ⲛ̄ⲕⲁⲣⲡⲟⲥ 'where are the fruits?' (Sh. 73.3.9); ⲉⲥⲧⲱⲛ ⲧⲁⳘⲟⲧⲉ 'where is my fear?' (Besa 17.22); ⲉⲩⲧⲱⲛ ⲡⲁⲉⲟⲟⲩ 'where is my honour?' (Besa 17.21).

100 Of the remainder, ⲁ⳩ⲣⲟ= , ϣⲁⲧⲛⲁⲩ and ϣⲁⲛⲧⲉ ⲟⲩ normally stand at the beginning of the sentence, exx. ⲁ⳩ⲣⲟⲕ ⲕ̄⳩ⲏⲡ 'why are you hiding?' (Sh. 42.38.18); ϣⲁⲧⲛⲁⲩ †ⲛⲁ ϣⲱⲡⲉ ⲛ̄ⲙ̄ⲙⲏⲧⲛ̄ 'how long shall I be with you?' (Mt. 17.17); ϣⲁⲛⲧⲉ ⲟⲩ ϣⲱⲡⲉ ⲉⲓⲉⲓⲣⲉ ⲛ̄ⲛⲓ⳩ⲃⲏⲩⲉ 'how long am I to perform these deeds?' (Besa 32.33).

Rarely, ⲁ⳩ⲣⲟ= can come after the verb, which, however, does <u>not</u> take a second tense, e.g. ⲁⲕⲟⲩⲟⲙ⳯ ⲟⲛ ⲁ⳩ⲣⲟⲕ ⲕ̄ⲥⲱϣ⳯ ⲙ̄ⲙⲟⲩ ⲁ⳩ⲣⲟⲕ 'why have you eaten it? why do you despise it?' (Sh. 73.85.9).

101 ⲉⲧⲃⲉ ⲟⲩ also normally stands at the beginning of the sentence, exx. ⲉⲧⲃⲉ ⲟⲩ ⲙ̄ⲡⲓⲥⲱⲧⲙ̄ 'why did I not hearken?' (Besa 38.21); ⲉⲧⲃⲉ ⲟⲩ ⲙ̄ⲡⲓⲉⲓ ⲉ⳩ⲣⲁⲓ 'why did I not come up?' (Besa 59.16). Occasionally it, too, can come after the verb, which in this instance takes a second tense, e.g. ⲛ̄ⲧⲁⲕⲉⲓ ⲉⲡⲉⲓⲙⲁ ⲉⲧⲃⲉ ⲟⲩ 'why have you come here?' (HM I 143.7).

102 ⲛⲓⲙ , ⲁϣ and ⲟⲩ are often followed by a relative substantive (§128), exx. ⲛⲓⲙ ⲡⲉⲧⲙ̄ⲡϣⲁ 'who is worthy?' (Mt. 10.11); ⲟⲩ ⲡⲉⲧⲛ̄ⲛⲁⲁⲁⲩ 'what shall we do?' (Jo. 6.28), lit. 'what is that which we shall do?'; ⲛⲓⲙ ⲡⲉⲛⲧⲁⲩⲉⲓ ⲉⲙⲁⲩ 'who came hither?' (Sh. 42.87.28), lit. 'who was the one who came hither?'; ⲁϣ ⲅⲁⲣ ⲡⲉⲧⲙⲟⲧⲛ̄ ⲉⲭⲟⲟⲥ 'which is easier to say?' (Mk. 2.9), lit. 'which

is that which is easier to say?'.

Otherwise ⲛⲓⲙ and ⲁⳉ follow the verb when used in a compound phrase. ⲟⳋ normally follows the verb even if used independently, exx. ⲉⲓⲛⲁϯ ⲟⳋ ⲛⲁⲕ 'what shall I give you?' (Gen. 30.31); ⲉⲧⲉⲧⲛ̄ⳉⲓⲛⲉ ⲛ̄ⲥⲁ ⲛⲓⲙ 'for whom are ye seeking?' (Jo. 18.4); ⲉⲓⲛⲁϫⲟⲟⲥ ⲛⲏⲧⲛ̄ ⲟⳋ 'what shall I say to you?' (Besa 31.14).

103 ⲛ̄ⲁⳉ ⲛ̄ϩⲉ can precede or follow the verb, exx. ⲛ̄ⲁⳉ ⲛ̄ϩⲉ ⲁⲕⲉⲓⲙⲉ 'how do you know?' (Cha. 41.36); ⲉⲧⲉⲧⲛ̄ⲛⲁϫⲟⲟⲥ ⲛ̄ⲁⳉ ⲛ̄ϩⲉ 'how will you say?' (Sh. 42.15.21).

104 The most important point to remember about these interrogative pronouns and adverbs is that when they come after the verb this will take a second tense. Of the exceptions to this rule ⲁϩⲣⲟ⸗ has already been noted. ⲟⳋⲏⲣ can take either a first or second tense, exx. ⲡⲁⲓ ⲣ̄ ⲟⳋⲏⲣ ⲛ̄ⲛⲟⲃⲉ 'how many sins does this one commit?' (Cha. 33.26); ⲉⲕⲛⲁⲣ̄-ⲙⲟⲉⲓϩⲉ ⲛ̄ⲟⳋⲏⲣ 'how much shalt thou wonder?' (Sh. 73.189.12). Finally, when ⲣ̄-ⲟⳋ is used with a Present tense this is sometimes the 1st Present, e.g. ⲛⲉⲛⲉⲓⲟⲧⲉ ⲉⲧϩⲛ̄ⲕⲏⲙⲉ ⲣ̄-ⲟⳋ 'what are our fathers in Egypt doing?' (Cha. 31.23).

105 In non-verbal sentences the interrogative word stands at the beginning of the sentence, except when ⲛⲓⲙ is used with an independent pronoun, which then precedes, exx. ⲛ̄ⲧⲕ̄ ⲛⲓⲙ 'who are you?' (Jo. 1.22); ⲟⳋ ⲡⲉ ⲡⲉⲓⳉⲁϫⲉ 'what is this word?' (Jo. 7.36); ⲛⲓⲙ ⲡⲉ ⲡⲣⲱⲙⲉ 'who is the man?' (Besa 51.22); ⲁⳉ ⲡⲉ ⲡⲉⲧⲛ̄ϩⲙⲟⲧ 'what is your thanks?' (Lk. 6.33); ϩⲉⲛ ⲉⲃⲟⲗ ⲧⲱⲛ ⲛⲉ ⲛⲓⲡⲟⲗⲉⲙⲟⲥ 'whence are these wars?' (Besa 28.9).

106 B When there is no interrogative word two methods of expressing the question are possible:
a) by the context, there being no other indication that a question is being posed, exx. ϯⲛⲁⲙⲟⲟⳋⲧϥ̄ 'shall I kill him?' (Sh. 42.26.21); ⲡⲉⲧⲛ̄ⲥⲛⲟⳋ ⲙⲛ̄ⲡⲉⲧⲛ̄ⲕⲣⲓⲙⲁ ⲉϩⲣⲁⲓ ⲉϫⲱⲛ 'are your blood and your condemnation upon us?' (Besa 119.8); ⲛ̄ⲧⲟⲕ ⲡⲉ ⲡⲣ̄ⲣⲟ ⲛ̄ⲛ̄ⲓⲟⳋⲇⲁⲓ 'are you the king of the Jews?' (Mt. 27.11)

b) more commonly, by means of an interrogative particle set at the beginning of the question.

107   There are three of these interrogative particles:

i) ⲈⲚⲈ ; normally used in questions requiring an answer, exx. ⲈⲚⲈ ⲔⲞⲨⲰϢ ⲈⲂⲰⲔ ⲈⲌⲢⲀⲒ ⲈⲐⲒⲈⲢⲞⲨⲤⲀⲖⲎⲘ   'do you wish to go up to Jerusalem?' (Acts 25.20); ⲈⲚⲈ ⲌⲈⲚⲘⲞⲚⲀⲬⲞⲤ ⲚⲈ ⲚⲀⲒ Ⲏ ⲈⲚⲈ ⲚⲀⲒ ⲚⲈ Ⲛ̄ⲢⲰⲘⲈ Ⲛ̄ⲀⲠⲀ ϢⲈⲚⲞⲨⲦⲈ   'are these monks', or 'are these men of Apa Shenute?' (Besa 63.14); ⲈⲚⲈ ⲈⲜⲈⲤⲦⲈⲒ Ⲙ̄ⲠⲢⲰⲘⲈ ⲈⲚⲈⲬ ⲦⲈⲨⲤⲌⲒⲘⲈ ⲈⲂⲞⲖ   'is it lawful for man to divorce his wife?' (Mk. 10.2)

ii) ⲘⲎ ; used in rhetorical questions, exx. ⲘⲎ ⲠⲀⲖⲀⲞⲤ ⲀⲚ ⲚⲈ ⲚⲀϢⲎⲢⲈ 'are they not my people, my children?' (Besa 59.30); ⲘⲎ ⲞⲨⲚϬⲞⲘ ⲈⲦⲢⲈⲞⲨⲂⲰ Ⲛ̄ⲔⲚ̄ⲦⲈ ⲦⲀⲨⲈ ⳚⲞⲈⲒⲦ ⲈⲂⲞⲖ 'can a fig tree bring forth olives?' (Besa 98.12); ⲘⲎ Ϯ ⳚⲰ ⲀⲚ Ⲛ̄ⲚⲀⲒ ⲌⲚ̄ⲞⲨϢϢⲰⲦ ⲈⲂⲞⲖ   'do I not say these things sharply?' (Sh. 73.6.16); ⲘⲎ ⲄⲀⲢ ⲈⲨ-ⲌⲒⲞⲨⲀⲢⲒⲤⲦⲞⲚ   'are they at a banquet?' (Besa 36.12).

If a negative is present the answer 'yes' is implied. If there is no negative the answer 'no' would be expected.

When emphasis is placed on an adverbial expression a second tense is employed, ⲘⲎ preceding the verb (see Polotsky, Études, p. 31, §9), exx. ⲘⲎ Ⲛ̄ⲦⲀⲨⲂⲰⲔ ⲈⲌⲢⲀⲒ ⲈⲦⲠⲈ   'is it to heaven that he has gone?' (Sh. 42.120.7); ⲘⲎ Ⲛ̄ⲦⲀⲨⲚ̄ⲦⲞⲨ ⲈⲂⲞⲖ ⲌⲘ̄ⲠⲈⲔⲎⲒ 'is it from thy house that they have been brought?' (Sh. 42.80.19).

iii) ⲈⲒⲈ ; this is also normally used in rhetorical questions, though occurring less frequently than ⲘⲎ , exx. ⲈⲒⲈ ⲚⲈⲦⲚⲀⲨ ⲈⲂⲞⲖ ⲚⲈⲦⲚⲀⳚⲚ̄Ⲉ Ⲛ̄ⲂⲖ̄ⲖⲈⲈⲨ ⲈⲚⲈⲌⲒⲞⲞⲨⲈ 'are those who see those who shall ask the blind the way?' (Sh. 42.49.21); ⲈⲒⲈ Ⲙ̄ⲠⲔ̄ⲤⲰⲦⲘ̄ Ⲛ̄ⲦⲞⲔ Ⲱ ⲠⲢⲰⲘⲈ   'have you not heard, O man?' (Besa 84.19); ⲈⲒⲈ ⲞⲨⲔⲞⲨⲚ ⲦⲚ̄ⲚⲀⲨⲒ ⲦⲈⲒⲘⲚ̄ⲦⲀⲐⲎⲦ ⲈⲂⲞⲖ Ⲙ̄ⲘⲞⲚ ⲀⲚ   'shall we not then put away from us this senselessness?' (Besa 8.8).

108   The Greek interrogative particles ⲁⲣⲁ or ⲏ are sometimes found at the beginning of questions, exx. ⲏ ⲛⲉⲓ2ⲃⲏⲅⲉ ⲁⲛ   'is it not these things?' (Besa 86.9); ⲏ ⲛ̄ⲧⲁⲛⲭⲟⲟⲅⲕ ⲛ̄ⲟⲩ2ⲱⲃ   'is it on a mission that we sent you?' (Besa 94.4); ⲁⲣⲁ ⲛⲁⲛⲟⲩ ⲡⲁⲧⲁⲙⲁⲁⲩ 'is my mother's way of life good?' (Cha. 55.32).

109   Double questions are linked by ⲭ(ⲓ)ⲛ or ⲏ , exx. ⲛ̄ⲧⲟⲕ ⲡⲉⲧⲛⲏⲩ ⲭⲛ̄ ⲉⲛⲛⲁϭⲱⲩⲧ̄ 2ⲏⲧϥ̄ ⲛ̄ⲕⲉⲟⲩⲁ 'are you the one who is to come, or is it for another we shall look?' (Lk. 7.19); ⲙⲏ ⲛ̄ⲧⲉⲧⲛⲁⲣ̄-2ⲟⲧⲉ ⲁⲛ 2ⲏⲧϥ̄ ⲙ̄ⲡⲭⲟⲉⲓⲥ ⲏ ⲛ̄ⲧⲉⲧⲛⲁⲩⲗⲁ2 ⲁⲛ ⲙ̄ⲡⲉϥⲙ̄ⲧⲟ ⲉⲃⲟⲗ 'will you not fear the Lord, or will you not be in awe before him?' (Besa 58.11).

EXERCISE VII
Vocabulary

ⲁ2ⲟⲙ	Sigh, groan; ⲁⲩⲁ2ⲟⲙ Groan, yawn, roar (m) (C. 655a)
ⲃⲗ̄ⲗⲉ	Blind person; ⲣ̄-ⲃⲗ̄ⲗⲉ Be, become blind
ⲅⲁⲗⲓⲗⲁⲓⲟⲥ	Galilean; ⲅⲁⲗⲓⲗⲁⲓⲁ Galilee (f)
ⲅⲁⲣ	For
ⲕⲏⲙⲉ	Egypt; ⲣⲙ̄ⲛ̄ⲕⲏⲙⲉ Egyptian
ⲗⲩⲡⲏ	Grief, sorrow (f)
ⲙⲛ̄ⲧⲣⲙ̄ⲛ̄2ⲏⲧ	Wisdom (C. 715a)
ⲥⲓⲱⲛ	Sion
ⲉⲡⲓⲥⲧⲓⲙⲏ	Understanding (f)
ⲓⲁⲕⲱⲃ	Jacob
ⲗⲁⲟⲥ	People (m)
ⲡⲉⲧⲣⲟⲥ	Peter
2ⲏⲃⲉ	Grief, mourning (m or f); ⲣ̄-2ⲏⲃⲉ To grieve (C. 655a)
2ⲕⲟ, 2ⲕⲁⲉⲓⲧ⁺	Be hungry
2ⲣⲁⲃⲃⲉⲓ	Rabbi

A English into Coptic

1 Simon Peter said to him: 'O Lord, whither are you going?'

2 Why did you not bring him?

3 O Lord, when did we see thee hungry?

4 Who is this Son of man?

5 Do I not fill heaven and earth?

6 They were saying to him: 'where is thy father?

7 How did he open your eyes?

8 He asked: 'is the man a Galilean?'

9 Is this not Jesus, the son of Joseph?

10 Art thou greater than (§ 87a) our father Jacob?

11 They said to him: 'Rabbi, at what time did you come here?'

12 No-one said 'what do you seek?' or 'why are you speaking with her?'

B Coptic into English

1 ⲡⲭⲟⲉⲓⲥ, ⲉⲛⲛⲁⲃⲱⲕ ϣⲁ ⲛⲓⲙ

2 ⲉⲣⲉ ⲛⲁⲓ ⲛⲁϣⲱⲡⲉ ⲧⲛⲁⲩ

3 ⲟⲩⲏⲣ ⲡⲉ ⲡⲉⲙⲕⲁϩ ⲛ̄ϩⲏⲧ ⲙⲛ̄ⲧⲗⲩⲡⲏ ⲙⲛ̄ⲡⲁϣⲁϩⲟⲙ

4 ϣⲁⲧⲛⲁⲩ ⲡⲕⲁϩ ⲛⲁⲣ̄-ϩⲏⲃⲉ

5 ⲉⲥⲧⲱⲛ ⲧⲙⲛ̄ⲧⲣⲙⲛ̄ϩⲏⲧ ⲉⲥⲧⲱⲛ ⲧⲉⲡⲓⲥⲧⲓⲙⲏ ⲉⲥⲧⲱⲛ ⲑⲟⲧⲉ ⲙ̄ⲡⲛⲟⲩⲧⲉ

6 ⲡⲉϫⲉ ⲡⲓⲗⲁⲧⲟⲥ ⲛⲁⲩ ϫⲉ ⲟⲩ ⲧⲉ ⲧⲙⲉ

7 ⲡⲉϫⲉ ⲛⲏ ⲛⲁⲥ ϫⲉ ⲧⲉⲥϩⲓⲙⲉ, ⲁϩⲣⲟ ⲧⲉⲣⲓⲙⲉ

8 ⲛⲁϣ ⲛ̄ϩⲉ ϥ̄ϫⲱ ⲙ̄ⲙⲟⲥ ϫⲉ ⲛ̄ⲧⲁⲓⲉⲓ ⲉⲃⲟⲗ ϩⲛ̄ⲧⲡⲉ

9 ⲉⲓⲉ ⲛ̄ⲧⲟⲕ ⲁⲛ ⲡⲉ ⲡⲣⲙ̄ⲛ̄ⲕⲏⲙⲉ

10 ⲙⲏ ⲙ̄ⲙⲛ̄ ⲙⲛ̄ⲧⲥⲛⲟⲟⲩⲥⲉ ⲛ̄ⲟⲩⲛⲟⲩ ϩⲙ̄ⲡⲉϩⲟⲟⲩ

11 ⲙⲏ ⲁⲛⲟⲛ ϩⲱⲱⲛ ϩⲉⲛⲃⲗ̄ⲗⲉ

12 ⲙⲏ ⲅⲁⲣ ⲛ̄ⲧⲁϩⲉⲛⲣⲱⲙⲉ ⲉⲓ ⲉϩⲟⲩⲛ ⲉⲣⲟⲛ

13 ⲙⲏ ⲡⲭⲟⲉⲓⲥ ϣⲟⲟⲡ ⲁⲛ ϩⲛ̄ⲥⲓⲱⲛ ⲏ ⲙⲛ̄ ⲣ̄ⲣⲟ ϣⲟⲟⲡ ⲙ̄ⲙⲁⲩ

14 ⲛ̄ⲧⲉⲧⲛ̄ⲥⲱⲧⲙ̄ ⲁⲛ ⲉⲡⲭⲟⲉⲓⲥ ⲡⲛⲟⲩⲧⲉ ⲉⲩϫⲱ ⲙ̄ⲙⲟⲥ ⲛ̄ⲛ̄ϣⲏⲣⲉ ⲙ̄ⲡⲓⲏⲗ

15 ⲏ ⲟⲩ ⲛⲟϭ ⲛ̄ⲛⲟⲃⲉ ⲁⲛ ⲡⲉ

XV CONDITIONAL SENTENCES (T. § 447ff)

110 These consist of two parts. Part A is the suppositional clause, the PROTASIS. Part B is the consequence clause, the APODOSIS. A normally precedes B.

Broadly, conditional sentences in Coptic can be placed under two headings, based on the nature of the suppositional clause:

A Real Conditional Sentences

B Artificial Conditional Sentences

111 A <u>Real Conditional Sentences</u>

The supposition in the protasis is feasible, as opposed to B below. There are a number of ways in which a Real Conditional sentence can be introduced:

a) by ⲉⲣϣⲁⲛ ; this form is made up of the prefixes of the Circumstantial Present (or possibly 2nd Present) + ϣⲁⲛ (see R. Kasser in <u>Le Museon</u>, Vol. 76, p. 267ff). The form before a nominal subject is ⲉⲣϣⲁⲛ , <u>not</u> ⲉⲣⲉϣⲁⲛ .

The commonest use of this construction is to express a supposition whose consequence will occur in the future, exx. ⲉⲣϣⲁⲛ ⲟⲩⲁ ⲃⲱⲕ ⲉϩⲟⲩⲛ ϩⲓⲧⲟⲟⲧ ϥⲛⲁⲟⲩϫⲁⲓ 'if one enters in by me he will be saved' (Sh. 42.60.5); ⲕⲛⲁϣⲡ̄ϩⲙⲟⲧ ⲅⲁⲣ ⲉⲣϣⲁⲛ ⲟⲩⲁ ϫⲟⲟⲥ ⲛⲁⲕ ϫⲉ ϫⲁⲓⲣⲉ 'for thou shalt give thanks if one says to you 'welcome'' (Sh. 42.101.5); ⲉⲧⲉⲧⲛ̄ϣⲁⲛⲕⲱ ⲅⲁⲣ ⲉⲃⲟⲗ ⲛ̄ⲛ̄ⲣⲱⲙⲉ ⲛ̄ⲛⲉⲩⲛⲟⲃⲉ ϥⲛⲁⲕⲱ ϩⲱⲱϥ ⲛⲏⲧⲛ̄ ⲉⲃⲟⲗ ⲛ̄ϭⲓ ⲡⲉⲧⲛ̄ⲉⲓⲱⲧ ⲉⲧϩⲛ̄ ⲙ̄ⲡⲏⲩⲉ 'for if you forgive men their sins your Father who is in heaven will forgive you also' (Mt. 6.14).

One also finds ⲉⲣϣⲁⲛ employed in more general suppositions, with time settings other than the future. On these occasions the apodosis can contain one of a number of tenses, most commonly the Habitude, Present or Perfect, exx. ⲉⲛϣⲁⲛⲉⲓⲣⲉ ⲅⲁⲣ ⲛ̄ⲧⲙⲉ ⲁⲛⲧⲁⲓⲉⲧⲙⲉ 'for if we are truthful we have honoured truth' (Sh. 42.112.25); ⲉⲣϣⲁⲛⲡⲉϥϩⲙ̄ϩⲁⲗ ⲣ̄-ⲃⲗ̄ⲗⲉ .... ⲙⲉϥⲕⲁⲁϥ ⲉⲉⲓ ⲙ̄ⲡⲉϥⲙ̄ⲧⲟ ⲉⲃⲟⲗ 'if his servant is blind .... he does not allow him to come before him' (Sh. 42.36.8); ⲉⲩϣⲁⲛⲣ̄-ⲁⲛⲁϣ ⲛ̄ⲛⲟⲩϫ ⲥⲉⲣⲱϣⲉ 'if they swear falsely they are responsible' (Sh. 42.17.25).

The apodosis can be non-verbal, e.g. ⲉⲧⲉⲧⲛ̄ϣⲁⲛϯ ⲉⲙⲏⲥⲉ .... ⲁϣ ⲡⲉ ⲡⲉⲧⲛ̄ϩⲙⲟⲧ 'if you give at interest .... what is your thanks' (Sh. 42.65.11).

ⲉⲣϣⲁⲛ is negated by ⲧⲙ̄ , which is normally placed after ϣⲁⲛ . A variant of this negative form, ⲉϥⲧⲙ̄- , with the ϣⲁⲛ element omitted, is apparently simply an older form (Kasser, op. cit., p. 269): exx. ⲉϥϣⲁⲛⲧⲙ̄ϫⲉ ⲡⲉⲧⲉϣϣⲉ 'if he does not say what is fitting' (Sh. 42.121.21); ⲉϥⲧⲙ̄ⲣⲟⲉⲓⲥ ⲙ̄ⲛⲉⲍⲃⲏⲩⲉ ⲡⲛⲟⲃⲉ ⲛⲁϣⲟⲗϥ̄ 'if he does not keep the works sin will destroy him' (Sh. 73.24.24); ⲉϥϣⲁⲛⲧⲙ̄ⲥⲱⲣ̄ ⲛ̄ϣⲟⲣⲡ̄ ⲛ̄ⲛⲉϥⲧⲱⲗⲙ̄ 'if its stains are not swept away first' (Sh. 73.192.7).

b) ⲉⲣϣⲁⲛ can be preceded by ⲉⲩϣⲱⲡⲉ , ⲉⲩϫⲉ , ⲍⲟⲧⲁⲛ or ⲕⲁⲛ . ⲍⲟⲧⲁⲛ ⲉⲣϣⲁⲛ invariably has a temporal meaning (§ 119). ⲕⲁⲛ ⲉⲣϣⲁⲛ is used in a concessive clause (§ 115). The other two constructions seem to be purely stylistic variants of ⲉⲣϣⲁⲛ. ⲉⲩϣⲱⲡⲉ and ⲉⲣϣⲁⲛ can be separated by other words: exx. ⲉⲩϣⲱⲡⲉ ⲉⲛϣⲁⲛⲧⲙ̄ⲥⲱⲧⲙ̄ ⲛ̄ⲥⲁ ⲡⲛⲟⲙⲟⲥ ⲙ̄ⲡⲛⲟⲩⲧⲉ 'if we do not obey the law of God' (Sh. 42.125.14); ⲉⲩϫⲉ ⲉⲩϣⲁⲛⲧⲙ̄ϯ ⲛⲉⲍ ⲛ̄ⲥⲁ ⲍⲉⲛⲍⲏⲃⲉ̄ ..... ⲙⲉⲩϫⲉⲣⲟ 'if they do not give oil to lamps ..... they do not burn' (Sh. 42.170.18); ⲉⲩϣⲱⲡⲉ ⲡⲍⲩⲡⲟⲕⲣⲓⲧⲏⲥ ⲉⲕϣⲁⲛϫⲓ ⲡⲣⲟⲕⲟⲡⲏ ⲍⲱⲥ ⲙⲟⲛⲁϫⲟⲥ 'if, O hypocrite, you receive advancement as (a) monk' (Sh. 42.141.12).

On the construction ⲉⲩϣⲱⲡⲉ ⲉⲣϣⲁⲛ see D. Young in J.N.E.S., Vol. 21 (1962), p. 175ff.

c) ⲉⲩϣⲱⲡⲉ can be found independently introducing a conditional sentence. Quite often it is simply replacing ⲉⲣϣⲁⲛ , especially when the protasis is non-verbal, exx. ⲉⲩϣⲱⲡⲉ ⲡⲟⲩⲱϣ ⲙ̄ⲡⲛⲟⲩⲧⲉ ⲡⲉ 'if it is the will of God' (Acts 18.21); ⲉⲩϣⲱⲡⲉ ⲟⲩⲡⲟⲣⲛⲟⲥ ⲡⲉ 'if he is a fornicator' (Sh. 42.192.22); ⲉⲩϣⲱⲡⲉ ⲕⲟⲩⲱϣ ⲁⲙⲁⲍⲧⲉ ⲙ̄ⲙⲟⲓ 'if you wish to restrain me' (Sh. 42.145.28).

d) ⲉⲩϫⲉ is often used independently to introduce a real conditional sentence. It can be followed by a non-verbal clause or by one of a number of tenses - Perfect (1st or 2nd), 1st Habitude, 1st Present, the Suffix Conjugation, or tenses with ⲛⲉ- . The apodosis can contain a question, wish, or instruction, in addition to a straightforward statement: exx. ⲉⲩϫⲉ ⲛ̄ⲧⲉ ⲟⲩⲙⲁⲁⲩ ⲇⲉ ⲟⲛ ⲛ̄ⲥⲁⲃⲏ 'if you are a wise mother' (Sh. 42.22.20); ⲉⲩϫⲉ ϣⲁⲣⲉ ⲡⲥⲁⲧⲁⲛⲁⲥ ⲧⲁⲕⲉ ⲡⲣⲱⲙⲉ 'if Satan destroys man' (Sh. 42.190.20); ⲉⲩϫⲉ ⲛⲁⲛⲟⲩⲉⲓ ⲕⲟⲓⲛⲱⲛⲉⲓ ⲛⲙⲙⲁⲓ 'if I am good, have dealings with me' (Sh. 42.30.19); ⲉⲩϫⲉ ⲛⲧⲛⲛⲁϣϣⲗⲏⲗ ⲁⲛ ⲉⲝⲛⲱⲝⲛ ⲙⲁⲣⲛϣⲗⲏⲗ ⲕⲁⲧⲁ ⲧⲛϭⲟⲙ 'if we find ourselves unable to pray without ceasing, let us pray according to our ability' (Sh. 42.27.28).

It is difficult to give a precise set of circumstances where ⲉⲩϫⲉ would be used rather than any of the other conditional constructions. It does not have the same strong future sense as conditional sentences employing ⲉⲣϣⲁⲛ frequently possess, but it seems as though the uses of the two constructions to some extent overlap, e.g. ⲉⲩϫⲉ ⲡⲉⲕⲃⲁⲗ ⲥⲕⲁⲛⲇⲁⲗⲓⲍⲉ ⲙⲙⲟⲕ 'if thine eye offends thee' (Mt. 18.9), and the same passage in Mk. 9.47 - ⲉⲣϣⲁⲛ ⲡⲉⲕⲃⲁⲗ ⲥⲕⲁⲛⲇⲁⲗⲓⲍⲉ ⲙⲙⲟⲕ.

ⲉⲩϫⲉ can be preceded by ϩⲱⲥ , normally with the meaning 'as if', e.g. ϩⲱⲥ ⲉⲩϫⲉ ⲟⲩⲥⲱϣ ⲛⲁⲩ ⲡⲉ 'as if it is a shame for them' (Sh. 42.36.1).

112 B Artificial Conditional Sentences

In sentences of this type a hypothetical supposition is proposed, more or less for the sake of argument, which cannot possibly be fulfilled. The protasis is introduced by ⲉⲛⲉ . When the protasis is verbal ⲉⲛⲉ can be followed by the 2nd Perfect (in affirmative clauses), the negative 1st Perfect, or coalesce to form a tense resembling the circumstantial imperfect, i.e. ⲉⲛⲉⲓ- , ⲉⲛⲉⲕ- , ⲉⲛⲉⲩ- , etc. The apodosis normally contains the Future Imperfect: exx. ⲉⲛⲉⲩⲥⲟⲟⲩⲛ ⲛϭⲓ ⲡϫⲟⲉⲓⲥ ⲙⲡⲏⲓ ..... ⲛⲉⲩⲛⲁⲕⲁⲁⲩ ⲁⲛ ⲉϭⲱⲧϩ ⲉⲡⲉⲩⲏⲓ 'if the master of the house had known ..... he would not have let them break into his house' (Lk. 12.39); ⲉⲛⲉ ⲛϣⲏⲣⲉ ⲛⲉ ⲙⲡⲉⲛϣⲣⲡ ⲛⲉⲓⲱⲧ ⲛⲉⲩⲛⲁⲣ ⲛⲉⲩϩⲃⲏⲩⲉ ⲡⲉ 'if they were children of our first father, they would have done his works' (Sh. 42.118.19); ⲉⲛⲉ ⲙⲡⲟⲩⲣⲡⲉⲧⲑⲟⲟⲩ ⲅⲁⲣ ⲛⲉⲩⲛⲁⲃⲱⲕ ⲉⲡⲧⲁⲕⲟ 'if they had not done wickedness would they have gone to perdition?' (Besa 61.8).

If the apodosis is a non-verbal sentence with nominal predicate, or an existential sentence, the simple Imperfect is used.

113   <u>Notes on Conditional Sentences</u>

ⲈⲒⲈ , 'then', often introduces the apodosis. In artificial conditional sentences ⲈϢⲬⲠⲈ (sometimes ⲈϢⲬⲈ or ⲈϢⲬⲈⲠⲈ) occasionally has the same function, exx. ⲈϢⲬⲈ Ⲙ̄ⲠⲈⲠⲈⲬ̄Ⲥ̄ ⲦⲰⲞⲨⲚ ⲈⲒⲈ Ⲥ̄ϢⲞⲨⲈⲒⲦ Ⲛ̄ϬⲒ ⲦⲈⲦⲚ̄ⲠⲒⲤⲦⲒⲤ 'if Christ did not arise then your faith is empty' (I Cor. 15.17); ⲈⲚⲈ Ⲛ̄Ⲧⲁ Ⲛ̄ϬⲞⲘ ⲈⲚⲦⲀⲨϢⲰⲠⲈ Ⲛ̄ϨⲎⲦ-ⲦⲎⲨⲦⲚ̄ ϢⲰⲠⲈ ϨⲚ̄ ⲦⲨⲢⲞⲤ ⲘⲚ̄ ⲤⲒⲆⲰⲚ ⲈϢⲬⲠⲈ ⲀⲨⲘⲈⲦⲀⲚⲞⲈⲒ 'if the mighty works, which were done in you, had been done in Tyre and Sidon, then they (would) have repented' (Mt. 11.21). Note the use of the 1st Perfect after ⲈϢⲬⲠⲈ instead of the Future Imperfect, a common construction under these circumstances.

114   Both Ⲛ̄ⲤⲀⲂⲎⲖ ⲬⲈ and ⲈⲒⲘⲎⲦ(Ⲉ)Ⲓ can be used to express 'unless', the latter often being followed by the Conjunctive tense (§ 71c) e.g. Ⲛ̄ⲤⲀⲂⲎⲖ ⲬⲈ ⲦⲚ̄ϢⲒⲠⲈ ϨⲀⲦϤ̄ Ⲙ̄ⲠⲂⲀⲖ ⲤⲚⲀⲨ 'unless we revere the two eyes' (Sh. 42.118.13).

115   A concessive clause ('although', 'even if') can be introduced by ⲔⲀⲒⲠⲈⲢ , ⲔⲀⲒⲦⲞⲒ , or ⲔⲀⲚ ⲈⲢϢⲀⲚ . Less commonly ⲔⲀⲚ ⲈϢⲬⲈ is used: exx. ⲔⲀⲚ ⲈⲨϢⲀⲚⲢ̄-ⲞⲨⲀⲚⲀϢ Ⲙ̄ⲘⲎⲚⲈ 'even if they swear an oath daily' (Sh. 42.19.28); ⲔⲀⲚ ⲈⲨϢⲀⲚϤⲒ Ⲛ̄ⲦⲈⲔⲀⲠⲈ Ⲕ̄ⲚⲀⲦⲰⲞⲨⲚ ⲞⲚ ⲈⲤϨⲒⲬⲰⲔ 'even though your head is removed thou shalt arise again with it upon thee' (Sh. 42.106.1).

116   'Whether ..... or' can be expressed by repetition of ⲔⲀⲚ , ⲈϢⲰⲠⲈ or ⲈⲒⲦⲈ , exx. ⲈϢⲰⲠⲈ ⲈⲨⲚⲞϬ ⲠⲈ ⲈϢⲰⲠⲈ ⲞⲨⲔⲞⲨⲒ ⲠⲈ 'whether great or small' (Sh. 42.198.1); ⲔⲀⲚ ⲞⲨϨⲞⲞⲨⲦ ⲠⲈ ⲔⲀⲚ ⲞⲨⲤϨⲒⲘⲈ ⲦⲈ 'whether husband or wife' (Sh. 73.154.12); ⲈⲒⲦⲈ ϨⲞⲞⲨⲦ ⲈⲒⲦⲈ ⲤϨⲒⲘⲈ 'whether husband or wife' (Sh. 73.154.16).

EXERCISE VIII

Vocabulary

ⲁⲣⲓⲕⲉ	Blame, reproof (m); ϭⲛ̅ⲁⲣⲓⲕⲉ To blame, find fault
ⲁⲓⲧ(ⲉ)ⲓ	Entreat, ask
ⲇⲉ	But, and
ⲉⲛⲉⲍ	Eternity; <u>as adj.</u> Eternal: <u>as adverb</u> Forever (C. 57a)
ⲉⲓⲇⲱⲗⲟⲛ	Idol (m)
ⲡⲁⲣⲁⲕⲗⲏⲧⲟⲥ	Paraclete (m)
ⲧⲁⲉⲓⲟ, ⲧⲁⲉⲓⲉ-, ⲧⲁ(ⲉ)ⲓⲟ=, ⲧⲁⲉⲓⲏⲩ†	Honour, respect (C. 390b)
ⲟⲩϣⲏ	Night (f); ⲛ̅ⲧⲉⲩϣⲏ By night (also ϩⲛ̅ⲧⲉⲩϣⲏ)
ⲭⲱⲣⲡ̅	Stumble, trip; ⲭⲣⲟⲡ Obstacle, impediment (m);
ⲭⲓ ⲭⲣⲟⲡ	Stumble (C. 786a)

A   English into Coptic

1 If you (f) believe, you will behold the glory of God

2 If you had been here my brother would not have died

3 If you do not work beside me I will not give you your wages

4 Even though he dies, he will live

5 If he is a man of God he (i.e. God) hearkens unto him

6 If one eats from this bread he will live forever

7 If you had known you would not have condemned

8 If you love me you will keep my commandments

9 If you know these things, blessed are you if you do them

10 If you wish to live, take the reproofs to your heart

B   Coptic into English

1   ⲉⲣϣⲁⲛ ⲟⲩⲁ ⲙⲟⲟϣⲉ ϩⲙⲡⲉϩⲟⲟⲩ ⲙⲉϥϫⲓ ϫⲣⲟⲡ, ⲉⲣϣⲁⲛ ⲟⲩⲁ ⲇⲉ ⲙⲟⲟϣⲉ ϩⲛⲧⲉⲩϣⲏ ϣⲁϥϫⲓ ϫⲣⲟⲡ

2   ⲉⲛⲉ ⲛⲧⲁⲩⲥⲟⲩⲱⲛⲥ ⲅⲁⲣ ⲛⲛⲉⲩⲛⲁⲥ̄ⲣⲟⲩ ⲁⲛ ⲙ̄ⲡϫⲟⲉⲓⲥ ⲙ̄ⲡⲉⲟⲟⲩ

3   ⲉⲓⲧⲙ̄ⲃⲱⲕ ⲅⲁⲣ ⲙ̄ⲡⲡⲁⲣⲁⲕⲗⲏⲧⲟⲥ ⲛⲏⲩ ⲁⲛ ϣⲁⲣⲱⲧⲛ̄, ⲉⲓϣⲁⲛⲃⲱⲕ ⲇⲉ ϯⲛⲁⲧⲛ̄ⲛⲟⲟⲩϥ

4   ⲉϣⲱⲡⲉ ϭⲉ ⲉⲛϣⲁⲛⲱⲛϩ, ⲉϣⲱⲡⲉ ⲉⲛϣⲁⲛⲙⲟⲩ, ⲁⲛⲟⲛ ⲛⲁⲡϫⲟⲉⲓⲥ

5   ⲉϣϫⲉ ⲛ̄ϯⲉⲓⲣⲉ ⲁⲛ ⲛ̄ⲛⲉϩⲃⲏⲩⲉ ⲙ̄ⲡⲁⲉⲓⲱⲧ ⲙ̄ⲡⲣ̄ⲡⲓⲥⲧⲉⲩⲉ ⲉⲣⲟⲓ, ⲉϣϫⲉ ϯⲉⲓⲣⲉ ⲇⲉ ⲙ̄ⲙⲟⲟⲩ, ⲕⲁⲛ ⲉⲧⲉⲧⲛ̄ⲧⲙ̄ⲡⲓⲥⲧⲉⲩⲉ ⲉⲣⲟⲓ, ⲡⲓⲥⲧⲉⲩⲉ ⲉⲛⲉϩⲃⲏⲩⲉ

6   ⲉⲧⲉⲧⲛ̄ϣⲁⲛ ⲁⲓⲧⲉⲓ ⲛ̄ⲟⲩϩⲱⲃ ϩⲙ̄ⲡⲁⲣⲁⲛ ϯⲛⲁⲁⲁⲩ

7   ⲉϣⲱⲡⲉ ⲉⲩϣⲁⲛⲧⲙ̄ ⲥⲱⲧⲙ̄ ⲉⲩⲛⲁⲛⲟϫⲟⲩ ⲉⲃⲟⲗ

8   ⲉⲛⲉⲧⲉⲧⲛ̄ ⲙⲉ ⲙ̄ⲙⲟⲓ ⲛⲉⲧⲉⲧⲛⲁ ⲣⲁϣⲉ

9   ⲕⲁⲛ ⲉⲕϣⲁⲛⲧⲁⲓⲟⲩ ϩⲛ̄ ⲛⲉⲕϣⲁϫⲉ

10   ϩⲱⲥ ⲉϣϫⲉ ϩⲉⲛⲉⲓⲇⲱⲗⲟⲛ ⲛⲉ

11   ⲡϫⲟⲉⲓⲥ, ⲉϣϫⲉ ⲁⲕϥⲓⲧϥ̄ ⲁϫⲓⲥ ⲉⲣⲟⲓ

XVI   TEMPORAL CLAUSES (T. § 428)

117 a)   **Contemporaneous Temporal Clauses**

These can be expressed:

i)   by means of the Circumstantial Present tense (§ 76)

ii)   by means of ϩⲙ̄ⲡⲧⲣⲉ- (§ 83e)

iii) by means of ϫⲓⲛ + the Circumstantial Present prefixes,
      exx. ⲁϥϫⲟⲟⲥ ϫⲓⲛⲉϥⲟⲛϩ   'he said, while he was still alive'
      (Sh. 42.102.13); ϫⲓⲛⲉϥ ⲛ̄ϩⲏⲧⲉ ⲛ̄ⲧⲉϥⲙⲁⲁⲩ   'while he was still
      within his mother' (Sh. 73.28.19)

iv)   with the help of certain Greek conjunctions, especially ϩⲱⲥ ,
      ϩⲟⲥⲟⲛ , ⲉⲧⲓ and ϩⲟⲧⲁⲛ , exx. ⲙⲟⲟϣⲉ ϩⲟⲥⲟⲛ ⲟⲩⲛⲧⲏⲧⲛ̄ ⲡⲟⲩⲟⲉⲓⲛ
      'journey while you have the light' (Sh. 42.191.4); ⲉⲧⲓ ⲉⲣⲉ
      ⲡⲕⲁⲕⲉ ⲛ̄ⲃⲟⲗ   'while it was dark outside' (Jo. 20.1)

118 b) <u>Past Temporal Clauses</u>

    i) By means of the following special tense to render 'when .....
had happened':

Sing. 1 ⲛ̄ⲧⲉⲣ(ⲉ)ⲓ-   Pl. 1 ⲛ̄ⲧⲉⲣ(ⲉ)ⲛ-

      2m ⲛ̄ⲧⲉⲣ(ⲉ)ⲕ-
                     2 ⲛ̄ⲧⲉⲣ(ⲉ)ⲧⲛ̄-

      2f ⲛ̄ⲧⲉⲣⲉ-

      3m ⲛ̄ⲧⲉⲣ(ⲉ)ⲩ-

                     3 ⲛ̄ⲧⲉⲣⲟⲩ-

      3f ⲛ̄ⲧⲉⲣ(ⲉ)ⲥ-

Before nom. subject ⲛ̄ⲧⲉⲣⲉ-   Negation: ⲧⲙ̄ before verb

exx. ⲛ̄ⲧⲉⲣⲟⲩ ⲣ̄-ⲛⲟⲃⲉ 'when they had sinned' (Besa 7.30); ⲛ̄ⲧⲉⲣⲉ
ⲟⲩⲛⲟϭ ⲛ̄ϩⲓⲥⲉ ϣⲱⲡⲉ ϩⲙ̄ⲡⲕⲁϩ 'when a great calamity had occurred
in the land' (Besa 41.29).

    ii) By means of ⲙⲛ̄ⲛ̄ⲥⲁⲧⲣⲉ- (§83d)

   iii) By means of ϫⲓⲛ-+ the 2nd Perfect prefixes, coalesced into
the form ϫⲓⲛⲧⲁⲓ- , ϫⲓⲛⲧⲁⲕ- , ϫⲓⲛⲧⲁⲩ- , etc., with the meaning
'since', exx. ϩⲛ̄ⲧⲙⲉϩϲⲟⲉ ⲛ̄ⲣⲟⲙⲡⲉ ϫⲓⲛⲧⲁ ⲡⲉⲛⲉⲓⲱⲧ ⲛ̄ϩⲗⲗⲟ ⲙ̄ⲧⲟⲛ ⲙ̄ⲙⲟⲩ
'in the 6th year since our revered father died' (Besa 41.26);
ϣϥⲉ ⲛ̄ⲣⲟⲙⲡⲉ ϫⲓⲛⲧⲁⲓ ⲣ̄ ⲙⲟⲛⲁⲭⲟⲥ '(it is) 70 years since I became
a monk' (Cha. 7.2).

    iv) Occasionally ⲉⲡ(ⲉ)ⲓⲇⲏ can be employed in a Past Temporal clause,
e.g. ⲉⲡⲉⲓⲇⲏ ⲁⲓⲙⲟⲩⲧⲉ ⲉⲣⲱⲧⲛ̄ 'when I called unto you' (Besa 13.10).

119 c) <u>Future Temporal Clauses</u>

    i) By means of ϣⲁⲛⲧⲉ- (§ 68)

    ii) By means of the conditional construction ⲉⲣϣⲁⲛ .
Context alone must decide which is being used. There are many
occasions when either translation would be suitable, although
when ϩⲟⲧⲁⲛ precedes ⲉⲣϣⲁⲛ this can only be a temporal clause:
exx. ϩⲟⲧⲁⲛ ⲉϥϣⲁⲛⲣ̄-ⲛⲟⲃⲉ ⲙ̄ⲡⲉⲙⲧⲟ ⲉⲃⲟⲗ ⲙ̄ⲡϫⲟⲉⲓⲥ 'when he sins
before the Lord' (Sh. 73.129.2); ϩⲟⲧⲁⲛ ⲉϥϣⲁⲛⲧⲙ̄ⲟⲩⲁϩⲙⲉϥ ⲉϩⲣⲁⲓ
ⲉⲡⲛⲟⲃⲉ 'when he does not add to the sin' (Sh. 73.128.10).

XVII CAUSAL CLAUSES (T. § 427)

120 These can be introduced by ⲭⲉ , ⲉⲧⲃⲉ , ⲉⲧⲃⲉ ⲭⲉ or ⲉⲃⲟⲗ ⲭⲉ , followed
by any tense or non-verbal clause, exx. ⲉⲃⲟⲗⲭⲉ ⲁⲩⲕⲱⲧ ⲙ̄ⲡⲉ ⲩ ⲏ ⲓ ⲉ ⲍⲣⲁⲓ
ⲉ ⲝⲛ̄ⲧ ⲡⲉⲧ ⲣⲁ 'because he has built his house upon the rock' (Besa 11.23);
ⲉⲧⲃⲉ ⲭⲉ ⲁⲛⲣ̄ⲁⲧ ⲥ ⲱ ⲧ ⲙ̄ ⲛ̄ⲥ ⲱ ⲕ 'because we disobeyed you' (Besa 43.2);
ⲭⲉ ⲛ̄ⲧⲕ̄ ⲟ ⲩ ⲛ ⲟ ⲩ ⲧ ⲉ ⲛ̄ⲛ ⲁ ⲏ ⲧ 'because you are a merciful God (Besa 44.24).

XVIII FINAL CLAUSES (T. § 423)

121 These can be introduced:

i) as a simple final clause by ⲭⲉ 'that', exx. ϯⲙⲟⲕ ⲍ̄ ⲛ̄ⲍ ⲏ ⲧ
ⲍⲁ ⲣ ⲟ ⲓ ⲛ ⲙ̄ⲙ ⲏ ⲧ ⲛ̄ ⲭⲉ ⲧ ⲉ ⲧ ⲛ̄ⲧ ⲁ ⲕ ⲟ ⲛ̄ⲧ ⲉ ⲧ ⲛ̄ⲯ ⲩ ⲭ ⲏ 'I am grieved with you that
you destroy your soul' (Besa 56.11); ⲭ ⲓ ⲛ ⲉ ⲛ ⲉ ⲍ ⲙ̄ⲡ ⲛ̄ⲥ ⲱ ⲧ ⲙ̄ ⲭⲉ
ⲁ ⲍ ⲉ ⲛ ⲧ ⲟ ⲡ ⲟ ⲥ ⲭ ⲓ ⲣ ⲱ ⲙ ⲉ ⲛ̄ⲟ ⲩ 'we have never heard that convents treat
men ill' (Besa 55.30)

ii) with future import by means of ⲭⲉ or ⲭⲉ ⲕ ⲁ ⲥ , followed by the 3rd
Future or 3rd Future negative, less commonly by the 2nd Future,
exx. ⲭⲉ ⲕ ⲁ ⲥ ⲉ ⲛ ⲉ ⲥ ⲱ ⲧ ⲙ̄ ⲉ ⲣ ⲟ ⲟ ⲩ 'so that we may hearken unto them'
(Sh. 42.120.8); ⲭⲉ ⲕ ⲁ ⲥ ⲉ ⲕ ⲛ ⲁ ⲥ ⲛ̄ ⲑ ⲉ ⲛ̄ⲥ ⲱ ⲧ ⲙ̄ 'so that you may
learn how to listen' (Sh. 42.99.25); ⲭⲉ ⲛ̄ⲛ ⲉ ⲡ ⲧ ⲁ ⲕ ⲉ ⲧ ⲁ ⲍ ⲉ ⲧ ⲏ ⲩ ⲧ ⲛ̄
'so that the darkness may not overtake you' (Besa 73.25)

iii) by means of the Greek conjunctions ⲍ ⲱ ⲥ ⲧ ⲉ , ⲙ ⲏ ⲡ ⲱ ⲥ and ⲙ ⲏ ⲡ ⲟ ⲧ ⲉ
followed by the conjunctive tense (§ 71)

iv) by means of the simple or causative infinitives preceded by ⲉ-
(§§ 81 & 83)

v) by ⲍ ⲱ ⲥ ⲧ ⲉ the causative infinitive (§ 83g)

vi) occasionally ⲩ ⲁ ⲛ ⲧ ⲉ is used in such a way that it also expresses
'so that', e.g. ⲩ ⲁ ⲛ ⲧ ⲉ ⲡ ⲡ ⲟ ⲛ ⲏ ⲣ ⲟ ⲛ ⲁ ⲩ ⲁ ⲓ ⲍ ⲣ ⲁ ⲓ ⲛ̄ⲍ ⲏ ⲧ ⲛ̄ 'so that
the evil increased among us' (Besa 68.28)

XIX RELATIVE CLAUSES (T. §461ff)

122 This is an important aspect of Coptic grammar. Apart from its normal usage the relative construction helps to compensate for the comparative lack of true adjectives, as well as taking the place of the participial construction.

Broadly, relative clauses can be divided into two groups:

A Where the antecedent and the subject of the relative clause are identical, i.e. 'the man who .....'

B Where the antecedent and the subject of the relative clause are different, i.e. 'the man whom we saw', 'the place in which I was', etc.

123 A Antecedent and Subject of the Relative Clause Identical

The relative is expressed:

a) By means of a circumstantial construction (i.e. the Circumstantial Present tense or the circumstantial Є- (§75)).

   i) This is invariably the construction when the antecedent is undefined, exx. ογχορτος εμⲛ̄καρπος 'a plant which has no fruit' (Sh. 42.35.1); ογαγγελος εαчει εβολ ϩⲓⲧⲙ̄ⲡⲛογτε 'an angel who has come from God' (Sh. 42.38.19); ϩⲉⲛⲥⲛⲏγ εγϣⲧⲣ̄ⲧⲱⲣ 'brethren who are disturbed' (Besa 3.20); ϩⲉⲛⲧⲱⲙε εⲙⲉγⲣ̄-ⲁⲥ 'purses which do not grow old' (Besa 40.34); ογϩⲓⲏ εⲛⲁⲛογⲥ ⲁⲛ 'a way which is not good' (Besa 46.24); ϩⲱⲃ ⲛⲓⲙ εγϩⲛ̄ⲧⲥγⲛⲁⲅⲱⲅⲏ 'everything which is in the assembly' (Sh. 42.172.26).

   ii) The same construction is used with the Imperfect and 1st Habitude tenses, whether the antecedent is defined or undefined, exx. ⲡⲉⲥⲛⲁγ εⲙϣⲁγⲃⲱⲕ εⲡⲭⲁⲓε 'the two who used to go to the desert' (Sh. 73.173.26); ⲛ̄ⲣⲱⲙε ⲙⲉⲛ εⲙϣⲁϩε ϩⲛ̄ογⲛοⲃε 'the men who fall into sin' (Cha. 59.31); ογϩⲣ̄ⲏⲣε εⲙϣⲁγⲧⲁⲕο 'a flower that perishes' (Besa 63.31).

   Sometimes, however, the prefix before the 1st Habitude takes the form ετε-, exx. ⲛⲁⲓ ετεⲙⲉγⲥⲓ 'these which are not satisfied' (Sh. 42.184.19); ⲡⲕⲁϩ ετεϣⲁγⲭⲓ ⲙοογ 'the earth which receives water (Sh. 42.160.25).

iii) Tenses etc. preceded by ⲛⲉ-(§ 78) also take the same circumstantial relative prefix.

b) <u>By means of the Relative Prefix</u> (ⲉⲧ- , ⲉⲧⲉ- or (ⲉ)ⲛⲧ-)

The antecedent is normally defined.

   i) ⲉⲧ- : all tenses not taking one of the other forms of the relative prefix; affirmative non-verbal sentences with adverbial predicate; adjective-verbs (i.e. ⲛⲁⲛⲟⲩ- , ⲛⲁⲁ- , etc.) exx. ⲧⲉⲭⲁⲣⲓⲥ ⲙ̄ⲡⲛⲟⲩⲧⲉ ⲉⲧⲛⲙ̄ⲙⲁⲓ 'the grace of God that is with me' (St. A. 9.5); ⲡ̄ⲭⲓ ⲛ̄ϭⲟⲛϭ ⲉⲧϩⲛ̄ⲛⲉⲩϭⲓⲝ 'the iniquity which is in their hands' (Besa 45.17); ⲧⲁϭⲣⲟⲟⲙⲡⲉ ⲉⲧⲛⲉⲥⲱⲥ 'my beautiful dove' (Sh. 42.52.10); ⲛ̄ⲣⲱⲙⲉ ⲉⲧϣⲱⲛⲉ 'the men who are sick' (Sh. 73.55.17); ⲧⲥⲁⲧⲉ ⲉⲧⲛⲁⲟⲩⲱⲙ ⲛ̄ⲛ̄ϫⲁϫⲉ 'the fire which will devour the enemies' (Besa 8.14).

   ii) ⲉⲧⲉ- : before all negatives; ⲙ̄ⲡⲁⲧⲉ- ; ⲟⲩⲛ- ; ⲟⲩⲛⲧⲉ- ; non-verbal sentences with nominal predicate: exx. ⲛⲁⲓ ⲉⲧⲉ ⲟⲩⲛⲧⲁⲩ ⲙ̄ⲙⲁⲩ ⲛ̄ⲧⲉⲩⲡⲓⲥⲧⲓⲥ 'those who have their faith' (Besa 3.23); ⲡⲕⲁϩ ⲉⲧⲉⲙ̄ⲡⲩ̄ ϫⲓ ⲙⲟⲟⲩ 'the land which did not receive water' (Sh. 42.160.17); ⲡⲭⲟⲉⲓⲥ ⲉⲧⲉ ⲡⲉⲩⲱⲛϩ̄ ⲡⲉ 'the Lord, who is his life' (Besa 114.29); ⲧⲥⲏϥⲉ ⲙ̄ⲡⲉⲡⲛⲁ ⲉⲧⲉ ⲡϣⲁϫⲉ ⲡⲉ ⲙ̄ⲡⲛⲟⲩⲧⲉ 'the sword of the spirit, which is the word of God' (Sh. 73.17.1); ⲟⲩⲟⲛ ⲅⲁⲣ ⲛⲓⲙ ⲉⲧⲉⲙ̄ⲡⲁⲧⲟⲩ ⲥⲟⲩⲱⲛϥ̄ 'for everyone who does not yet know thee' (Sh. 42.77.26); ⲁⲩⲥⲱϣϥ̄ ⲙ̄ⲡⲁⲓ ⲉⲧⲉ ⲛ̄ϥ̄ⲙ̄ⲡϣⲁ ⲙ̄ⲙⲟϥ ⲁⲛ 'he despised this one who is unworthy of him' (Sh. 42.142.15).

   iii) (ⲉ)ⲛⲧ- : used only before the 1st Perfect affirmative, exx. ⲧⲟⲣⲅⲏ ⲉⲛⲧⲁⲥⲉⲓ ⲉϫⲙ̄ⲡⲗⲁⲟⲥ 'the wrath which has come upon the people' (Besa 10.5); ⲛ̄ϣⲏⲣⲉ ⲛ̄ⲓⲱⲛⲁⲇⲁⲃ ⲉⲛⲧⲁⲩϩⲁⲣⲉϩ ⲉⲛⲉⲛⲧⲟⲗⲏ ⲙ̄ⲡⲉⲩⲉⲓⲱⲧ 'the sons of Jonadab, who kept the commandments of their father' (Besa 10.3); ⲉⲛⲥⲱϣ ⲙ̄ⲡⲛⲟⲩⲧⲉ ⲉⲛⲧⲁⲩⲧⲁⲙⲓⲟⲛ 'we despise God, who made us' (Besa 17.29).

124 The examples in sections a) and b) above illustrate an important point. When the antecedent is nominal, and the relative clause contains a verb, adjective-verb, or ογΝΤε-, the antecedent is normally reiterated pronominally in the relative expression. Thus: ƍεΝτωμε εμεγρ̄-ας ; ταƍροομπε ετΝεςως ; ογƍρηρε εƍƍαγτακο etc. This rule does not apply, however, when the 1st Present and 1st Future tenses are prefixed by ετ- (see the examples in b) i)). Neither does it normally apply when ετ- precedes an affirmative non-verbal sentence with adverbial predicate (examples in b) i)). Very occasionally, however, the antecedent **is** reiterated in these circumstances, e.g. πκωƍτ̄ ετƍΝ̄ƍητ̄ƍ ƍραι ƍΝ̄αμΝ̄τε 'the fire which is in hell' (Besa 12.31).

125 Note the expression ετε παι πε, lit. 'which is this', used with the meaning 'in other words', 'that is to say', e.g. ceΝα† Ναƍ μ̄ποεικ ετε παι πε πΝομος μ̄πΝογτε 'he shall be given the bread, that is to say, the law of God' (Sh. 42.33.24).

126 On some occasions a choice of relative constructions seems possible. For example, in the sentence 'a man who did not go', the fact that the antecedent is undefined would suggest a circumstantial relative construction, while the negative would indicate that ετε- is required. Under these circumstances, and others similar, the fact that the antecedent is undefined is decisive, e.g. ογκωƍτ̄ εμεγωμ̄ 'a fire which is not quenched' (Sh. 42.63.18).

127 B <u>Antecedent and Subject of the Relative Clause Different</u>
On these occasions the antecedent is reiterated by a <u>resumptive pronoun</u>, which is underlined in the following examples.

Normally, the relative constructions described in section A remain unchanged, only the resumptive pronoun being inserted, exx. πεοογ εΝεγΝταιƍ 'the glory which I had (Jo. 17.5), lit. 'the glory which I had <u>it</u>'; πμα εΝτακβωκ εροƍ 'the place to which you went' (Besa 22.14), lit. 'the place which you went <u>to it</u>; πμα εΝεƍωοοπ Ν̄ƍητ̄ƍ 'the place in which he was' (Sh. 73.120.17), lit. 'the place which he was <u>in it</u>'; ƍεΝειοτε εαπΝογτε ϭοƍƍογ 'fathers whom God has humbled (Sh. 73.28.27), lit. 'fathers whom God has humbled <u>them</u>';

ⲠⲢⲰⲘⲈ ⲈⲚⲦⲀⲠϪⲞⲈⲓⲤ ⲠⲚⲞⲨⲦⲈ ⲦⲀⲘⲓⲟⲩ

'the man whom the Lord God has created' (Sh. 73.48.19), lit., 'the man whom the Lord God has created _him_'.

On the following occasions, however, the relative assumes a different form, though the resumptive is still necessary:

a) When the Present and Future tenses are employed the following forms are used:

Present				Future			
Sing. 1	ⲈϮ -	Pl. 1	ⲈⲦⲚ̄-	Sing. 1	ⲈϮⲚⲀ-	Pl. 1	ⲈⲦⲚ̄ⲚⲀ-
2m	ⲈⲦⲔ̄-			2m	ⲈⲦⲔⲚⲀ-		
2f	ⲈⲦⲈ-	2	ⲈⲦⲈⲦⲚ̄-	2f	ⲈⲦⲈⲚⲀ-	2	ⲈⲦⲈⲦⲚ̄ⲚⲀ-
3m	ⲈⲦϥ̄-			3m	ⲈⲦϥ̄ⲚⲀ-		
3f	ⲈⲦⲤ̄-	3	ⲈⲦⲞⲨ-	3f	ⲈⲦⲤ̄ⲚⲀ-	3	ⲈⲦⲞⲨⲚⲀ-

Before nom. subject ⲈⲦⲈⲢⲈ-　　　　Before nom. subject ⲈⲦⲈⲢⲈ .....ⲚⲀ

exx. ⲠⲘⲞⲞⲨ ⲈϮⲚⲀⲦⲀⲁⲩ Ⲛⲁϥ　　'the water which I shall give him' (Jo. 4.14); ⲚⲈϨⲂⲎⲨⲈ ⲈϮⲈⲓⲢⲈ Ⲙ̄Ⲙⲟⲟⲩ　　'the works which I do' (Jo. 5.36); ⲠⲀⲅⲀⲐⲟⲚ ⲈⲦⲈⲢⲈ ⲠⲞⲨⲀ ⲠⲞⲨⲀ ⲀⲨⲰ ⲦⲞⲨⲈⲓ ⲦⲞⲨⲈⲓ ⲚⲀⲀⲁⲩ 'the good which each man and each woman shall do' (Besa 21.20); ⲠⲘⲀ ⲈⲦⲤ̄ⲚⲀϬⲰϢⲦ̄ ⲈⲢⲟϥ　　'the place towards which she shall look' (Sh. 73.17.12); ⲠⲚⲞⲘⲞⲤ ⲈⲦⲞⲨϢⲀϪⲈ ⲈⲦⲂⲎⲎⲦϥ̄　'the law concerning which they speak' (Sh. 73.8.18); ⲠⲘⲀ ⲈⲦⲈⲢⲈ ⲚⲈⲤⲚⲎⲨ ⲦⲎⲢⲞⲨ ⲤⲞⲞⲨϨ Ⲛ̄ϨⲎⲦϥ̄ 'the place in which all the brethren gather' (Sh. 73.120.12).

b) These forms are also used in affirmative non-verbal sentences with adverbial predicate, exx. ⲠⲀⲓ ⲈⲦⲈⲢⲈⲠⲈϥϨⲀ ϨⲚ̄ⲦⲈϥϬⲓϪ　　'this one, in whose hand is his fan' (Mt. 3.12); ⲠⲎⲒ ⲈⲦϥ̄ Ⲛ̄ϨⲎⲦϥ̄　　'the house in which he is' (Sh. 73.44.26); Ⲙ̄ⲘⲀ ⲈⲦⲞⲨⲚ̄ϨⲎⲦⲞⲨ　'the places in which they are' (Sh. 73.56.20).

c) In non-verbal sentences with nominal predicate, and often in negative non-verbal sentences with adverbial predicate, the circumstantial prefix Ⲉ- is used, exx. ⲠϨⲈⲐⲚⲞⲤ ⲈⲠϪⲞⲈⲓⲤ ⲠⲈ ⲠⲈϥⲚⲞⲨⲦⲈ 'the nation whose God is the Lord' (Ps. 32.12); ⲠⲀⲓ ⲈⲚϮⲘ̄ⲠϢⲁ ⲀⲚ Ⲛ̄ⲂⲰⲗ Ⲙ̄ⲠⲘⲞⲨⲤ Ⲙ̄ⲠⲈϥⲦⲞⲞⲨⲈ　　'this one, the thong of whose sandal I am unworthy to untie' (Lk. 3.16).

d) Adjective-verbs are preceded by ⲈⲦⲈ- ; exx. ⲠⲒϢⲰⲚⲈ ⲈⲦⲈ ⲚⲀϢⲈ ⲦⲈϥϨⲘ̄ⲘⲈ 'this sick man, whose fever is great' (Sh. 73.19.10);

ⲡϩⲁⲣⲙⲏϩⲏⲧ ⲉⲧⲉⲛⲁϣⲉ ⲡⲉϥⲛⲁ 'the falcon, whose mercy is great' (Sh. 42.84.15).

128 A relative expression can be preceded by a <u>definite</u> article to form a substantive. As substantives they in turn can be preceded by other articles, possessives, etc: exx. ⲁⲣⲓ ⲡⲙⲉⲉⲩⲉ ⲛ̄ⲛⲉⲛⲧⲁⲓ ϫⲟⲟⲩ 'remember what I have said' (Sh. 42.21.2), lit. 'the things which I said'; ⲕⲁⲧⲁ ⲡⲉⲛⲧⲁⲩⲉⲓ ⲉⲃⲟⲗ ϩⲛ̄ⲧⲟⲩⲧⲁⲡⲣⲟ 'according to what has come out of your mouth' (Besa 39.8); ⲡⲉⲧⲛⲁⲙⲉⲣⲉ ⲡⲡⲉⲑⲟⲟⲩ 'whosoever shall love evil' (Besa 39.19); ⲕⲁⲧⲁ ⲡⲉⲧⲥⲏϩ 'according to what is written' (Sh. 42.116.11); ⲉⲩⲙⲉ ⲙ̄ⲡⲡⲉⲑⲟⲟⲩ ⲛ̄ϩⲟⲩⲟ ⲉⲡⲡⲉⲧⲛⲁⲛⲟⲩϥ 'loving evil more than good' (Sh. 42. 19.19), lit. 'loving that which is evil more than that which is good'.

RELATIVE CLAUSES – SUMMARY TABLE

ANTE-CEDENT	TENSE etc.	ANTECEDENT & SUBJECT SAME				ANTECEDENT & SUBJECT DIFFERENT	
		Є-	ЄT-	ЄTЄ-	(Є)NT-	RELATIVE PREFIX	
D E F I N E D	Present		X			Єϯ- etc.	R E S U M P T I V E P R O N O U N
	Future		X			Єϯна- etc.	
	Imperfect	X				No change	
	Habitude	X	or	X		" "	
	Perfect				X	" "	
	Non-Verbal Sentence with Nominal Predicate			X		Є-	
	Affirmative Non-Verbal Sentence with Adverbial Predicate		X			Єϯ- etc.	
	Negative Non-Verbal Sentence with Adverbial Predicate			X		Often Є-	
	Other Negatives			X		No change	
	NЄ- Constructions	X				" "	
	OYN-			X		" "	
	OYNTЄ-			X		" "	
	Adjective Verbs		X			ЄTЄ-	
UNDE-FINED	Verbal or Non-Verbal: Use the Circumstantial Є- or the Circumstantial Present Tense					The Relative Prefix Є- does not change	

<u>Note</u> The resumptive pronoun is occasionally omitted when the antecedent and subject of the relative clause are different and the antecedent is an expression of time, place or manner, e.g. м̄пнаY ЄтN̄нашшнЄ 'at the time when we shall fall ill' (Sh. 73.78.8).

Vocabulary

ⲙⲟⲩⲣ, ⲙⲉⲣ-, ⲙⲟⲣ=, ⲙⲏⲣ⁺   Bind, tie (C. 180a)

ⲣⲱⲕ⳰ⲍ, ⲣⲉⲕ⳰ⲍ-, ⲣⲟⲕ⳰ⲍ=, ⲣⲟⲕ⳰ⲍ⁺   Burn

ⲥⲱⲗⲡ̄, ⲥⲗⲡ̄-, ⲥⲟⲗⲡ̄=, ⲥⲟⲗⲡ̄⁺   Break, cut off

ⲥⲩⲛⲁⲅⲉ   Administer communion

ⲧⲃ̄ⲃⲟ, ⲧⲃ̄ⲃⲉ-, ⲧⲃ̄ⲃⲟ=, ⲧⲃ̄ⲃⲏⲩ⁺   Become, be pure; purify; ⲧⲃ̄ⲃⲟ Purity (m)
(C. 399b)

ⲧⲁ(ⲟ)ⲩⲟ, ⲧⲁⲩⲟ-, ⲧⲁ(ⲟ)ⲩⲟ=   Send

ⲱϣⲙ̄, ⲉϣⲙ̄-, ⲟϣⲙ̄=, ⲟⲩϣⲙ̄⁺   Be quenched, quench ·

ⲧⲱⲕⲙ̄, ⲧ(ⲉ)ⲕⲙ̄-, ⲧⲟⲕⲙ̄=, ⲧⲟⲕⲙ̄⁺   Pluck, draw, drag

ϭⲗⲟⲙⲗⲙ̄, ϭⲗⲙ̄ⲗⲱⲙ-, ϭⲗⲙ̄ⲗⲱⲙ=, ϭⲗⲙ̄ⲗⲱⲙ⁺   Be twisted, implicated

ϭⲱⲱⲙⲉ, ϭⲉ(ⲉ)ⲙⲉ-, ϭⲟⲟⲙⲉ⁺   Be twisted, crooked

ⲕⲣⲁⲛⲓⲟⲛ	Skull (m)	ⲟⲩⲟⲛ	Someone, something;
ⲗⲁⲍⲁⲣⲟⲥ	Lazarus	ⲟⲩⲟⲛ ⲛⲓⲙ	Everyone
ⲙⲟⲛⲁⲭⲟⲥ	Monk; ⲙⲟⲛⲁⲭⲏ Nun	ϣⲗⳍ	Twig, shoot (m)
ⲣⲏⲥ	South (m); ⳍⲁⲣⲏⲥ	ⳍⲏⲩ	Profit, usefulness (m);
(or ϣⲁⲣⲏⲥ)	To the south	ϯ-ⳍⲏⲩ	Give profit (C. 729a)
ⲥⲟⲩⲇⲁⲣⲓⲟⲛ	Napkin (m)	ϭⲱⲙ	Garden (m)
ⲧⲱⳍ	Chaff (m)	ⲡⲣⲉⲥⲃⲩⲧⲉⲣⲟⲥ	Priest (m)
ⲡⲟⲩⲁ ⲡⲟⲩⲁ	Each one (C.469b)		

A English into Coptic

1 The garden which Jacob gave to Joseph his son

2 The napkin which was bound upon (ⲉ-) his head

3 This one who opened the eyes of the blind man

4 The works which I do in the name of my Father

5 The place in which John was baptizing

6 I will go unto my Father, who is thy father, and my God, who is thy God

7 For everyone who has, unto him shall be given

8 The works which another did not do

9 Whatever he shall say unto you, do it

10 Come (pl) and behold a man who has told you ('said unto you')
the truth

11 Everyone who shall drink from this water, he shall not thirst

12 This one (f) whose brother Lazarus was ill

13 This man whom they call Jesus

14 This multitude which knows not the law

15 This is the will of him who sent me

16 He does not honour the Father who sent him

17 This, which the Son of man will give you

18 But you, O brethren, who fear God and who love purity, blessed
are you

19 He is a blind man who does not see

20 All those who have died

B   **Coptic into English**

1 ϣⲗⲏⲗ ⲛⲓⲙ ⲉⲧⲉ ⲛϥ̄ⲛⲁϯⲕⲁⲣⲡⲟⲥ ⲁⲛ ϥ̄ⲛⲁⲥⲟⲗⲡϥ̄, ⲁⲩⲱ ϣⲗⲏⲗ ⲛⲓⲙ ⲉⲧⲛⲁϯ ⲕⲁⲣⲡⲟⲥ ϥ̄ⲛⲁⲧⲃ̄ⲃⲟϥ

2 ⲡⲉⲧⲛⲁ ⲥⲱ ⲉⲃⲟⲗ ⲙ̄ⲡⲙⲟⲟⲩ ⲉϯⲛⲁⲧⲁⲁϥ ⲛⲁϥ ⲛ̄ⲛⲉϥⲉⲓⲃⲉ

3 ⲡⲙⲁ ⲉϣⲁⲣⲉ ⲛ̄ⲓⲟⲩⲇⲁⲓ ⲧⲏⲣⲟⲩ ⲥⲱⲟⲩϩ ⲛ̄ϩⲏⲧϥ̄

4 ⲛⲉϥⲣ̄ ⲙⲛ̄ⲧⲣⲉ ⲛ̄ϭⲓ ⲡⲙⲏⲏϣⲉ ⲉⲧⲛ̄ⲙ̄ⲙⲁⲩ

5 ⲧⲛ̄ϭⲗⲟⲙⲗⲙ̄ ϩⲛ̄ⲛⲉⲓϩⲃⲏⲩⲉ ⲉⲧϭⲟⲟⲙⲉ, ⲉⲧⲉ ⲙⲛ̄ϩⲏⲩ ⲛ̄ϩⲏⲧⲟⲩ

6 ⲁⲩⲉⲓ ⲉⲃⲟⲗ ⲉⲩⲙⲁ ⲉⲩⲙⲟⲩⲧⲉ ⲉⲣⲟϥ ϫⲉ ⲡⲉⲕⲣⲁⲛⲓⲟⲛ

7 ⲛⲉϩⲃⲏⲩⲉ ⲅⲁⲣ ⲉⲛⲧⲁⲡⲁⲉⲓⲱⲧ ⲧⲁⲁⲩ ⲛⲁⲓ ϫⲉⲕⲁⲥ ⲉⲓⲉϫⲟⲕⲟⲩ ⲉⲃⲟⲗ, ⲛ̄ⲧⲟⲟⲩ
ⲛⲉϩⲃⲏⲩⲉ ⲉϯⲉⲓⲣⲉ ⲙ̄ⲙⲟⲟⲩ

8 ⲡⲉⲡⲣⲉⲥⲃⲩⲧⲉⲣⲟⲥ ⲉⲧⲛⲁⲥⲩⲛⲁⲅⲉ ⲛ̄ⲛⲉⲥⲛⲏⲩ ⲉⲧϩⲁⲣⲏⲥ, ⲉⲧⲉ ⲙ̄ⲙⲟⲛⲁⲭⲏ ⲛⲉ

9 ⲡϣⲁϫⲉ ⲉⲧⲉⲧⲛ̄ⲥⲱⲧⲙ̄ ⲉⲣⲟϥ ⲙ̄ⲡⲱⲓ ⲁⲛ ⲡⲉ ⲁⲗⲗⲁ ⲡⲁⲡⲉⲓⲱⲧ, ⲡⲉⲛⲧⲁⲩⲧⲁⲅⲟⲓ

10 ⲁⲛⲟⲕ ⲡⲉ ⲡⲟⲉⲓⲕ ⲉⲧⲟⲛϩ̄, ⲉⲛⲧⲁⲩⲉⲓ ⲉⲃⲟⲗ ϩⲛ̄ⲧⲡⲉ

11 ⲡⲙⲁ ⲉⲛⲉⲣⲉ ⲡⲥⲱⲙⲁ ⲛ̄ⲓ̄ⲥ̄ ⲛ̄ϩⲏⲧϥ̄

12 ⲡⲉϩⲟⲟⲩ ⲛ̄ⲧⲟⲣⲅⲏ, ⲉⲧⲉ ⲡⲉϩⲟⲟⲩ ⲡⲉ ⲉⲧⲟⲩⲛⲁⲧⲱⲕⲙ̄ ⲛ̄ⲧⲉⲯⲩⲭⲏ ⲙ̄ⲡⲟⲩⲁ ⲡⲟⲩⲁ

13 ⲕⲁⲧⲁ ⲡⲉⲛⲧⲁ ⲡϫⲟⲉⲓⲥ ϫⲟⲟⲩ

14 ⲡⲧⲱϩ ⲉⲧⲟⲩⲛⲁⲣⲟⲕϩϥ̄ ϩⲛ̄ⲟⲩⲕⲱϩⲧ̄ ⲉⲙⲉϥϣⲱⲙ̄

15 ⲡⲙⲁ ⲉⲧⲉⲣⲉ ⲡⲉⲧⲙⲟⲟⲩⲧ ⲕⲏ ⲉϩⲣⲁⲓ ⲛ̄ϩⲏⲧϥ̄

XX NEGATION

129 Throughout this grammar, the various ways in which Coptic negates verbal and non-verbal sentences and phrases have been noted. A summary
is given below.

a) By means of special negative auxiliaries – 1st Perfect; 1st
Habitude; 3rd Future

b) By means of ⲧⲙ̄- the Simple and Causative Infinitives; the
Prospective Conditional; the Conjunctive; the Past Temporal;
the Potential Future; ϣⲁⲛⲧⲉ-; ϩⲙ̄ⲡⲧⲣⲉ-

c) ⲙ̄ⲡⲣ̄- – the Optative; the Imperative

d) By means of ⲛ̄ .....ⲁⲛ , the ⲛ̄ often being omitted – all
tenses not possessing a special negative auxiliary; non-verbal
sentences and phrases; adjective-verbs

e) ⲉⲛ .....ⲁⲛ – the Circumstantial Present

INDICES

1 English

Abbreviations	§ 2b)	Linking of Sentences	§ 71
Absolute Forms	§§ 8, 50a), 93	Oaths	§ 58
Abstract Nouns	§ 24a)	'Perfect Continuous' meaning	§ 58
Adverbs	§§ 24c), 74, 81b), 96	Prohibition	§§ 63, 79
Apodosis	§ 110ff.	Pronominal Forms	§§ 50a), 93
Change of Consonants	§ 3a)	Protasis	§ 110ff.
Coalescing of Consonants	§ 3a)	Resumptive Pronoun	§ 127
Comparison	§ 87a)	Rhetorical Question	§§ 107ii), iii)
Construct Forms	§§ 8, 32, 42a), 50b), 93	Second Tenses	§§ 74, 99, 101, 104, 107iii)
Contraction	§§ 4, 5, 24	Semi-Consonants	§§ 3b), 19b)
Copula	§§ 41-44	Sonant Consonants	§ 3 p. 2, § 20
Dative	§§ 87a), 99	Subordinate Clauses	§§ 75-77
Dialects	p. iv	Verbal Prefix	§ 57
Dual Nouns	§ 16	Vocative	§ 22c)
Emphasis	§§ 8, 9, 42, 43, 74, 81b), 90ff.	Vowels	§ 4
		'Whether .... or'	§ 116
Greek Verbs	§ 95	Wishes	§§ 63, 66

2 Coptic and Greek

ⲁⲩⲱ 'And'	§§ 71, 73	(ⲉ)ⲛⲧ- Relative prefix	§ 123b)
ⲁⲣⲁ Greek interrogative particle	§ 108	ⲉⲣϣⲁⲛ- In conditions	§ 111
ⲁⲧ- Negative Prefix	§ 17c)	In temporal clauses	§ 119ii)
ⲇⲉ 'But, and'		ⲉⲧ- Relative prefix	§ 123b)
ⲉ- Circumstantial prefix	§§ 75, 123a)	ⲉⲧⲉ- Relative prefix	§ 123b)
Introducing indirect objects	§ 94	ⲉⲓⲧⲉ 'Or'	§ 116
ⲉⲓⲉ In questions	§ 107iii)	(ⲉ)ϣ 'Be able'	§ 85
In conditions	§ 113	ⲉϣⲱⲡⲉ In conditions	§ 111b) & c), 116
ⲉⲓⲙⲏⲧ(ⲉ)ⲓ 'Unless'	§§ 71c), 114	ⲉϣⲭⲉ In conditions	§ 111d)
ⲉⲛⲉ Interrogative particle	§ 107i)	ⲉϣϫⲡⲉ In conditions	§ 113
Conditional particle	§ 112		

ⲔⲈ   'Other'   § 31

ⲔⲀⲚ   In concessive clauses §§ 115, 116

ⲘⲎ   Interrogative particle   § 107ii)

(ⲙ̄)ⲙⲛ̄   'There is not' §§ 44, 55, 58, 62

ⲘⲚ̄Ⲧ-   Noun prefix   § 17c)

Ⲙ̄ⲠⲈⲘⲦⲞ   'Before'   § 87c)

ⲘⲎⲠⲰⲤ   'Lest'   §§ 71c), 121iii)

ⲘⲎⲠⲞⲦⲈ   'Lest'   §§ 71c), 121iii)

ⲘⲀⲢⲞⲚ   'Let us go'   § 60

ⲘⲈⲌ-   Ordinal prefix   § 36ff

ⲚⲈ-   Plural copula   § 41ff

         Plural definite article   § 19

         Past prefix §§ 43, 78, 123a) iii)

ⲚⲀⲚⲞⲨ   Adjective-verb §§ 53, 123b) i)

Ⲛ̄ⲦⲀ=   Form of Genitive   § 26

Ⲛ̄ⲦⲈ-   Form of Genitive   § 26

Ⲛ̄ϬⲒ   'Namely'   § 91

Ⲡ Ⲉ   Masc. copula   §§ 41ff, 60, 67

         Masc. definite article   § 19

ⲠⲈϪⲈ-, ⲠⲈϪⲀ=   'Said'   § 53

ⲢⲈϤ-   Noun prefix   § 17d)

ⲤⲞⲨ   'Day'   § 38

ⲦⲈ   Fem. copula   § 41ff

         Fem. definite article   § 19

Ⲧⲙ̄   Negative element §§ 57, 65, 69, 72, 84, 111

ⲦⲎⲢ=   'All'   §§ 26, 27

ⲞⲨⲚ-   'There is' §§ 45, 54, 58, 62

ⲞⲨⲚⲦⲈ-   To have   §§ 55, 56, 124

Ⲍⲱⲥ   In conditions   § 111, p.66

         In temporal clauses 117iv)

ⲌⲞⲤⲞⲚ   In temporal clauses 117iv)

ⲌⲰⲤⲦⲈ   'So that'   §§ 71c), 83g), 121iii), iv)

ⲌⲒⲦⲚ̄-   Agent of passive   § 86

ⲌⲞⲦⲀⲚ   Temporal prefix § 117iv)

ϪⲈ   Introducing final clauses   §§ 63, 121

         Introducing speech   § 97

         Introducing causal clauses   § 120

ϪⲰ   'To say'   § 95

ϪⲈⲔⲀⲤ   Introducing final clauses   §§ 63, 121ii)

ϪⲒⲚ   Temporal prefix §§ 117iii), 118iii)